Rise Up and Remember

Rise Up and Remember

꒰✧⊹┈⊹✧꒱

Barbara Nauer

DOUBLEDAY & COMPANY, INC.
GARDEN CITY, NEW YORK
1977

Grateful acknowledgment is made to the publishers, authors, and copyright owners of works quoted in this book for permission to reprint excerpted materials. From "Design for a House" by Charles O'Donnell, *Collected Poems of Charles O'Donnell*, reprinted by permission of the University of Notre Dame Press. "The Hollow Men" by T. S. Eliot, *Collected Poems 1909–1962*, reprinted by permission of Faber and Faber, Ltd., and Harcourt Brace Jovanovich, Inc. "Song for a Listener" by Leonard Feeney, *The Leonard Feeney Omnibus*, published by Sheed & Ward, 1943. *Poems of Gerard Manley Hopkins*, W. H. Gardner and N. H. McKenzie, Editors, by permission of Oxford University Press.

Biblical excerpts from The Jerusalem Bible, copyright © 1966 by Darton, Longman & Todd, Ltd., and Doubleday & Company, Inc. Used by permission of the publishers.

Library of Congress Cataloging in Publication Data

Nauer, Barbara.
Rise up and remember.

1. Nauer, Barbara.   2. Catholic in the
United States—Biography.   3. Pentecostalism—
Catholic Church.   I. Title.
BX4705.N284A37   248'.2'0924 [B]

ISBN: 0-385-12955-6
Library of Congress Catalog Card Number 76–54011
Copyright © 1977 by Barbara Nauer
All Rights Reserved
Printed in the United States of America
First Edition

For Walter J. Ong, S.J.

Preface

I remember, and my soul
melts within me:
I am on my way to the wonderful Tent,
to the house of God,
among cries of joy and praise
and an exultant throng.

—Psalm 42–43:4

Like most Catholics of middle years, I have a warm feeling for the old hymn "Holy God, We Praise Thy Name." The song is all bound up with some of the happiest occasions of my growing up in the Church. One would sing the lusty anthem loudly at the close of High Mass, Benediction, and certain grand processions. On all sides would be relatives, classmates, and other persons from one's school or parish, booming more or less on key.

I always liked to linger in church for a while after the singing of "Holy God." Many times I have sat or knelt in reverent awe to watch the cloud of incense coil and rise and then flatten out lazily over the sanctuary. The incense always gave a dreamlike quality to the altar scene, as mists give to inland lakes at sunrise.

Sometimes I saw the tabernacle and the altar banked with roses or lilies glittering through my tears. I always knew that God had truly been present, after "Holy God."

Charismatic or pentecostal Christians believe in something called inner healing or "healing of the memories." They believe that if one turns to the Lord in full and expectant faith, he can and will miraculously heal not only bodily diseases and impairments but psychological illnesses too.

They firmly believe that the Lord, being unrestricted by time and space, can "go backwards" in time and put his healing touch on the raw and bleeding memories that underlie our present angers, anxieties, and fears.

In relation to the old hymn "Holy God," I personally have reason to believe that this process can be made to work in the opposite direction too. It appears that the Lord can also "come forward" in time, and that our beautiful, warm, and precious memories can serve as his avenues of entrance into our souls. I want to tell you my story.

It is a story about memories. The self that I am now, the one writing these lines, is remembering her self of nearly three years ago, a younger self who brooded over memories of her yet earlier selves in an effort to make some sense out of her life.

Now, it is well that I did so. For that which makes sense out of human life, which alone makes despair inappropriate, "rides time like riding a river," as the poet Hopkins said. In the river of time, in the flow of memory, our personal memories and those of all humanity, do we find the ultimate meaning of things—if we find it at all.

But I am ahead of myself. I intended merely to observe that each man and woman, of any age, is a child of memory, shaped by memory, nourished by it as by a womb. And so all spiritual healings, one way or another, involve a healing of the memories. On with my story.

Rise Up and Remember

CHAPTER ONE

It is like this
In Death's other kingdom
Walking alone. . . .

—T. S. Eliot

. . . And so I dare to hope,
Though changed, no doubt, from what I was when first
I came among these hills; when like a roe
I bounded o'er the mountains, by the sides
Of the deep rivers, and the lonely streams,
Wherever nature led. . . .

—William Wordsworth

My life almost ended a few years ago, on a bitter-cold night in mid-January. The time was between 1 and 2 A.M. I was working my third job, after being a public school teacher during the day and a part-time librarian for the evening.

I was serving as an unarmed security guard, unarmed because I was new to guard work and had not yet gone through training at the police academy. I was at my post on a deserted motel construction site not far from our city's outlying airport.

I had just walked one of our pair of police dogs on the required rounds, a stroll through the half-built units. I was seated behind a cluttered desk inside a mud-tracked house trailer that served as the contractor's field office during the days and our guard station after hours. I had nothing to do but stare glumly at the day's leavings—scrawled telephone messages, some greasy blueprint scrolls filled with wiring and plumbing specifications, and several work gloves that did not match. Underneath my coat, which I wore against the chill of the trailer, I was dressed in my policewoman's blue slack outfit. On my head was the visored uniform cap in which I always felt ugly and ridiculous.

The sounds of an engine and of tires crunching on frozen mud told me that our dumpy little sergeant was running a check on me. I quickly shoved out of sight a copy of *America* magazine that I had been disconsolately attempting to read since coming on duty at ten. I had been rapped by the sergeant once before for reading while on post.

Icy air came in the door with my visitor. He wore his cheap brass buttons like a breastplate of virtue and was bursting, as usual, with self-importance. I groaned inwardly against the upcoming half an hour or so of his arrogant and ignorant company. The sergeant's small talk was usually rawly flirtatious, though laced with gleeful, sadistic accounts—some of which I had heard several times—of his use of the dogs to corner young black thieves and vandals.

He proceeded in his customary way, squatting on a scarred metal stool that he tilted cockily against the wall to my left. Then at length he stood up, grunted, and proceeded to unbuckle his holster. He was getting ready, I saw, to go outside and attend to the dogs.

One part of me relaxed slightly. I knew it would take the sergeant at least fifteen minutes to feed and relocate the dogs so as to confound anyone "out there" who might be trying to establish exactly where in the units we kept the animals chained. But once he had gone out the door, another part of me grew strangely alert.

I stared at the shiny revolver, so unexpectedly dropped right in front of me. A sudden impulse set my thoughts to racing. My nerves tensed across my strained and aching shoulders. My thoughts had been so despairing before the sergeant entered, and for many days and nights previous to this one, that I felt urged, driven, the very instant that his back was turned, to use his pistol on myself.

It amazes me now as I write this that no pang for my children or thought for anyone else came into my mind in those moments. I was consumed by one thought only, from the instant the weapon landed so opportunely within my grasp. That was to have the whole long grinding nightmare of my life *over*. This truly can be said of a spirit that has been shorn of all its hopes and exhausted through overwork, and then is entered and possessed by wretchedness: its darkness and depression are total.

Realizing that I had plenty of time in which to get the brief grisly job over, I looked around me at the long, ugly vault of the trailer. I sat with my back to the end wall of the breakfast area and gazed through the kitchenette to the darkened far end. The double bunks at that end served as catchalls for junk from the job.

It was a grim scene. The trailer's walls were lined with muddy picks and shovels and workmen's galoshes. One of the overhead recessed lights blinked spasmodically. My attention returned to the gun, and I felt a deep ironical laugh coming. I wanted to throw back my head and let it out.

I recalled how in my teens I had decided against entering a Benedictine convent to which I had been attracted, one in Nauvoo, Illinois, because, as I told a close girl friend at the time, "The nuns' world seems so narrow." I, energetic and ambitious and talented I, wanted to travel and, even more, to write.

But now here I was, twenty-five years after that decision, with little of what had teemed in my brain written and with even less of it published, friend to at least a dozen nuns, a couple of them Nauvoo Benedictines, who had been to Europe more than once and spent their summers very creatively, studying in one university center after another around the U.S.A.

During this time I had managed only to locate in California for a few impoverished childbearing years, and I had been East only once. This precious trip East, to New York City, had been made almost ten years before, at the time of my most recent vacation in my nearly vacationless life.

Entombed in the dirty trailer, I half wished its glazed

walls would move in and down and conveniently complete the job of crushing me that life itself had been working on ever since my arrival at maturity.

Surveying the desk top in front of me, I sensed that if I moved my hand at all, I would go all the way with the gun. The itchy-fingered sergeant, I knew, always kept his gun loaded. I decided to sit quietly, composed, for some moments, before moving the hand.

The thought of the Nauvoo convent connected with and churned up other old memories. Brooding into the unlighted far end of the trailer, I seemed to stare down a long tunnel or corridor of time. The convent that had played a part in my adolescent decision was almost at the far end of this tunnel, with childhood memories lying beyond it, furthest of all from me. Something moved me to begin lining up my life's major events in sequence. I started at the near and bitter end, with the present.

Piled up in front of me on the desk top, like some once-beautiful but now shattered object, was my associate professorship. The bits and pieces of it represented the wiping out of some fifteen years of determined and serious professional effort, including three years of doctoral study in literature.

The ruination of my career in college teaching, I should explain, had occurred roughly two years before this time of my having the guard's job. In my life situation, which was that of a solitary breadwinner for a family, my loss of my professional status would have been distressing at the very least. But the setback was seen by me as disastrous, and permanently so, because of two circumstances.

The job market for college teachers, both at the time that I had lost my job and for the foreseeable future, was in such state of decline that for me to make a fresh start in academic life was out of the question. And the particular setback that I had sustained, a termination of my teaching contract at the point when I had become eligible for tenure, had happened in a set of circumstances so rare and ominous and, in terms of normal academic procedures, so irregular, that all the months since had not dulled or removed the shock of what had occurred.

On the stage of my memory, the main events and people who were part of what happened over many months of time came startlingly alive again. Like one in the act of viewing a play from a front-row seat, I saw my colleagues and students and myself detachedly but clearly. I saw us living out our roles in a setting surrounded by shadows, a place originally the campus of a public college but now, thanks to memory's way of locating events precisely nowhere, on some stage hung out in cosmic space.

Dread filled me as I sat there over the gun. I was alone, the only audience in a dark theater, and I was looking on close-up scenes that were chiefly memorable for showing the utter helplessness of ordinary men and women, teacher types, before the matchless cunning of a few trained subversives. The connivers involved, middle-class whites with foreign and far-left allegiances, had established themselves professionally in an urban public college with the all-consuming purpose of inciting the college's swelling minority student body to paranoid hatreds and class revolution.

My college reminiscences continued for some moments, and so rapt was I in my remembering of the confused and violent period at the school that I felt decidedly disoriented, upon "coming to" some moments later, to find myself still seated at the guards' desk with the shiny gun before me.

I could draw a direct line between the campus events and my hated job as a guard. There in the chilly and littered guards' trailer, I lived out the consequences of my having opposed the sinister plans of the revolutionist faction. Its leaders had been faculty colleagues of mine, and they had acted to have my tenure denied and my contract terminated. Since that time I had been forced to work at a variety of poorly paid professional positions or wretched sales and clerical jobs. My foremost need, one that by now I could see was hopeless of fulfillment, was to earn enough to meet my financial commitments. These included several installment loans and numerous other smaller obligations that I had contracted when times, which for me had never been good, were at least better and seemed likely to improve. I had no hope whatever of a return to academic life. Did the depressed job market not make my situation hopeless, my not having entirely completed the doctorate would.

My life seemed to be going past me in separate scenes now, like one of those medieval pageants of mystery and miracle plays that flowed past spectators with its individual scenes done by players on horse-drawn carts. There seemed no end to what might take form and shape in the memory tunnel. A good ten feet away from where the broken pieces of my professional career had set off the remembrances of the dark events at the college, a new vision arose.

This recollection took shape further away down the memory tunnel, rising up about where the bath and closets were in the center of the trailer. I saw my Catholic marriage at twenty to the first boy I had ever dated with any regularity, a young man easily as immature and uninformed as myself. Then on the near side of this I saw the births of our five children, one each year during the five years following.

The divorce that took place ten years after the start of

the marriage rose up a few feet closer to me than the children's births. Even down the distance of the dozen years between the collapse of the marriage and my trailer reminiscences, the divorce appeared like the surrealistic nightmare it had been at the time.

A host of presences I was pained to remember rose up with my recollections of the divorce period. There were the critical relatives, bored lawyers, cocksure psychiatrists, ineffectual parish priests, nosy acquaintances, and demanding creditors who appeared at the time when a human institution of sacred origin was collapsing from its own dead weight, though not without two-way desperation and some violence. These parties, acting largely out of self-interest, had interjected the devilish elements of blame and retribution.

On the near side of the divorce maelstrom I saw my emotionally battered and exhausted self, a young woman instructor in a Catholic university, just turned thirty, making $3,000 a year, hopelessly in debt, and with five small children to raise alone.

But then, as I sat there at my desk in the chilly trailer, my imagination, which was amusing itself with this memory play, suddenly found itself at a loss to summon shapes or faces to fill the space that lay roughly between the kitchenette, scene of the divorce, and the heaped-up desk top where I had just reviewed my final days as a college professor. This particular stretch of the past that I was gazing down, off to the front of the desk, had the appearance of a flat, barren void. But my heart shrank to recall what its individual days had felt like, scraping against my sensibility.

A good title for this eight-year stretch, which covered most of the years between the divorce and my loss of my teaching job, might have been "The Drag to the Ph.D."

But that would not have hinted at the desperate fight for solvency and the relentless clawing for financial security that beset every waking hour and most nights of this period. The pressures of this time distressed in numerous ways my relationship with my growing and needful children. I was always overburdened, tense, anxious over where our next car insurance payment—or the charges for heat, electricity, auto repairs, winter clothing, baby-sitter, dentist, and so on—were going to come from.

Nor would a title that covered those things have pointed to what, finally, had been the greatest trauma of this time. My faith died.

God disappeared first. One morning—it was while I was still married—when I knelt at the altar rail after daily Mass to storm heaven concerning the rapidly deteriorating relationship between my husband and me, God seemed to have vanished. The difference was as real as if a sign stood in the sanctuary, "Moved to a New Location."

My initial reaction had been to think that this phenomenon of God's disappearance was temporary, perhaps the result of strain. But it continued.

After that, gradually, my other religious certainties fell away. My deep attachment to the Church turned into rebellion and then, after I had found the time to sort out the broken pieces of my life, to rage. I eventually answered for myself the question with which I had been storming heaven on that day in church when even the Real Presence in the Blessed Sacrament, for which I had had a lifelong fascination, had seemed to disappear from the altar and my days: why had a marriage in which none of the usual causes of divorce had been present—alcoholism, infidelity, neglect, and so on—failed?

The answer was strikingly clear. It was hissed at me

daily out of the bright pink envelopes of creditors whose mounting bills lay in a frightening, seemingly radioactive, pile on my desk. The Church's inhuman and unyielding laws against sensible family planning, helped along by ordinary bad luck, had overburdened a grossly immature young couple with financial and other concerns that had driven both parties to desperation and distraction, and the male partner and the marriage union to total collapse.

Anger and outrage at the astounding callousness of the Church, whose officials had more recently turned down my application for annulment, gripped me afresh as I sat in the trailer contemplating all these things.

But a bothersome distraction occurred at this point. Although I considered myself to be minutes away from extinction, the artistic and literary side of me, which was determinedly composing this final review of my life, now began to feel distinctly bothered that, for all my trying, I could not assemble the appropriate images for the "Ph.D. drag," that waste of many prime years, that consumed the time between the divorce and the professional disasters at the college. This period simply would not take shape as scenes, as pictures, or as human activities to be contemplated.

Mentally I struggled. My self-pity started to rise. It was as if this summary recollection of my life's main scenes, somehow necessary if I were to die and escape from my misery as planned, were about to bog down. The entire review was going to come to a dead halt, it seemed, if I did not come up with some evocative or at least apt image or tableau or dramatization of the dreadful bleakness of those eight years following the divorce.

My irritation mounted. I tried this and that combination of the period's bits and pieces in my head, but all to no avail. Next I began to be sharply annoyed that even in these final minutes of my life I should be bedeviled by a special kind of suffering that I had known as far back as I could remember. This is the frustration that is laid on any artist or serious would-be artist who is held back from his or her craft by other people's blindness or the press of circumstances or some disastrous combination of the two.

"Even one's gifts are curses!" I raged this silently to myself there at the guards' desk. The howls of the police dogs at the slowness of their feeder were like the wails of my psyche against its chains. I thought about how many days of my childhood and adult life I had risen at 3, 4, or 5 A.M. in order to set words down on paper before duty, tormentor of my childhood and consumer of my maturity, had yanked me away from my stolen joy.

For the artist there is only one pain worse than not being able to get the pieces to fit, to "make the thing come out right." That is continually being prevented from trying. This I had learned a thousand times over. I railed over its being life's final teaching for me too.

While the police dogs snarled against their chains far back in the icy units, I struggled to bring some memory shapes to the dark void just off in front of me and representing so many wasted years of my adulthood. A mental picture finally began to emerge, but even as it came, the image struck me as strained and melodramatic. I saw myself as tied, like a beast of burden, to some strange, awkward conveyance. The thing was not right, was built freakishly, like a clumsy old cart but with square wheels. From another angle it seemed like an old-fashioned sleigh, but with no runners. My sole purpose was to pull it. But of course the whatever-it-was resisted all forward motion. At best, even with me bent double and straining to my limit, it inched, dragged. Around my ankles the vicious creditors ever sprang, snarling.

Although my artistic good taste told me that this picture was ridiculous, especially for a woman, perspiration slicked my forehead behind the band of the hated cap. I could feel one of my *Where is reality?* crises coming. For I had just foreseen that in order to complete the mental exercise I had started—and I had never been one to leave anything half-done—I would have to draw my eyes away from this spectacle of abject misery and futility and look, as well, into the deepest, furthest end of the tunnel, at my childhood.

I forcibly drew the gaze of my mind's eye in that direction now. My childhood rose up at the shadowy end of the trailer, bathed as in golden light. It shimmered and seemed infinitely long. My remembering seemed to have melted the far wall just beyond the bunks. My childhood appeared to me now like a vast long landscape with an end but with no definite beginning.

I recognized the golden setting as the woods and creeks —*cricks* the local people called them—and towering hillsides around my parents' rented old frame house in a tiny coal-mining town, Bartonville, some ten miles outside of Peoria.

We lived in the "hollow" section of Bartonville. The hollow included little more than an old winding road flanked by a few houses nestled between steep wooded hills. Bartonville's hollow had been to youthful me an enchanted land. Even at this distance and in these circumstances I marveled that my overprotective parents had let me, as a preschooler, wander those trackless woods and untenanted high places in the company of only our burr-ticked cocker spaniel. I had discovered that at one high point on the hills, a full mile from our home, I could see distant Peoria. On clear days I would fight my way upward and over fallen trees and through blackberry brambles in order to stand in awe, gazing at the faraway city. Seen through vapors rising from the lazy river and the breweries on her lower end, old Peoria would gleam like the heavenly Jerusalem.

Nor did I stop at looking, in my wonder world. From my earliest recollections in that lovely place, I had peopled the rocky creeksides and the grassy clearings between the great trees with the heroes of my daily radio programs and movies. My favorites were the Lone Ranger and Tonto and their mounts, Silver and Scout. But I also called upon Snow White and the Seven Dwarfs and upon Tarzan, who swung on the ropy vines that hung from the sun-dappled trees. I could make the woods echo with my Tarzan yell.

At least, this was how I continued until I was enrolled in school, which I was at age five because doting relatives had decided I was precocious. Then a new and different company came to share the secret paths I traveled to explore hidden springs and faraway hilltops. These parties assembled with me regularly at one of my favorite spots. It was by a small waterfall which had some great rocks where the dragonflies darted and the garter snakes sunned themselves in the summer and the ice assumed exciting shapes during the wintertime.

These friends were not made-up characters like the others. They were real, introduced to me by the Holy Cross nuns who prepared me for first Holy Communion at St. John's school in a parish on the Bartonville side of Peoria. The company included Our Lord and his Blessed Mother under dozens of titles and appearances, my guardian angel, and half a dozen or so favorite saints. They became my daily companions during hours when I was away from my school friends and my family or was otherwise alone. I talked and prayed to them all and sometimes, just as I had earlier joined the Lone Ranger and Tonto in their gallops over the hills, I re-enacted New Testament scenes with them.

There began at some point my special attraction for the Blessed Sacrament. When I started to use some of my recess and playtime at school to make visits in the parish church, or to remain in church after Benediction, my heavenly friends from the woods were presences before the altar with me.

In fact there grew in my child's mind some curious connection between still and darkened St. John's Church, where the red sanctuary lamp flickered by the altar, and the woodlands where I pursued my imaginative rambles. God and his saints were in both places, in a way that they were nowhere else. I never had occasion to tell anybody this, but I knew it.

There in the guards' trailer I had gone rigid at the sight of the loveliness that lay like a vision at the childhood end of my tunnel of time. My thoughts of the gun temporarily scattered. With something akin to physical pain, and with more clarity than I had remembered anything else, I saw myself as a child, rapt before the Blessed Sacrament. I seemed to hear again the strains of "Holy God," saw the incense rise in a ghostly cloud, and watched the tabernacle front and the rose sprays begin to glitter and flow.

"No!" I cried, grabbing the near edge of the heavy desk. "No!"

The outburst was less a denial of anything than a protest at having to confront, once again, the unbearable—unbearable because utterly mind-boggling—contrast between the radiant promise of my childhood and the adult realities that were the issue of it.

My *Where is reality?* demon had me by the throat.

Was life a carefree and adventuresome ramble, companioned by Christ and his mother and the saints, through a landscape lighted by God's love? Or was the truer, the more accurate, picture of life the one in which I saw myself bent nearly double, ringed by attackers, doomed to drag along by inches an impossible load, under dark and pitiless skies?

CHAPTER TWO

✤✥✦✥✤

That only is true enlargement of mind which is the power of viewing many things at once as one whole, of referring them severally to their true place in the universal system, of understanding their respective values, and determining their mutual dependence.

—John Henry Newman

. . . There is less difference than people think between research and adoration.

—Pierre Teilhard de Chardin

My brow behind the band of the cap felt slimy with sweat again, so I yanked the thing off. These fierce philosophical tugs of war invariably made my nerves feel as drawn as strained rubber bands. The recurrent *Where is reality?* agony, in which I found myself torn between two starkly contrasting views of human existence, always lasted for some minutes. That it involved intellectual suffering of great intensity was a result of my having been coached into an especially careful brand of scholarship during my graduate school years.

Among the competent to superior professors under whom I had studied at two different graduate schools, a Jesuit university and another fine private university, there had been one matchless scholar, a man of international renown in humanistic letters. He was a Jesuit professor of literature, a man as kind as he was brilliant, and he became, as well as my teacher and thesis director, my mentor and spiritual guide. My Jesuit teacher was a creative and prolific personality, and over the years some of the habits of his driving and original mind, one especially noted for its thoroughness, had rubbed off on me. Because of this man's influence, I always decided philosophical questions, even ones much less urgent than the one troubling me now, with great care.

But for the moment, finding myself sitting in that dingy trailer, with my mind feeling as if it were going to split from the tension of indecision, I was tempted to curse the day that I had fallen under the influence of this particular teacher. From somewhere in the time tunnel there came now his familiar voice, lecturing to one of our graduate

classes. I heard him once again making an offhand obser-
vation which, at the time he originally made it, had
struck me as worth remembering and thinking about.
"Even while we're writing up our last note card, reality is
squirting out at the edges. We never quite nail it down." I
had jotted it down in my class notes.

In another of the weird visions that were originating in
the time tunnel, I saw my priest-professor as of old, during this period of my studies, roughly the period before
my marriage problems began. In my recollection, he was
seated in his neatly organized faculty office, behind his
desk, in one of the somber old classroom buildings. He
was flanked by some potted plants that he was wont to
fuss over solicitously. He was murmuring aloud to me
while he sorted through some file slips of his own research notes.

On the other side of his desk was I, a young mother
taking occasional graduate courses, in the act of receiving
my favorite teacher's guidance in some research connected with a literary term paper. I was sitting there
amazed, as I had been on other occasions, by the care and
voluminousness of my mentor's note-taking. By this point
in his life he was using precut slips of bond paper, instead
of index cards, in an effort to cut down on bulk.

But on the occasion that I was remembering now,
something about my priest-professor had come to strike
me as vaguely eccentric, at once touching and slightly
comical. Even his potted greens looked neatly organized,
not like other people's house plants. They actually seemed
to bend intently, as my middle-aged adviser did, toward
the note slips that were neatly penned in his clear mascu-
line hand.

Sitting across from my professor that day, I had felt a
deep, full laugh coming. With amusement I saw myself,

exhausted from production of a research paper for one of his high-powered courses, trudging up and over a series of mountains of scholarship in the wake of my determined mentor. My Jesuit was indefatigable when he was in search of support for a promising insight or hypothesis. So serious students like myself who admired and tried to imitate him inevitably came to feel like followers of the bear that went over the mountain. On the highest peaks this bear would glimpse yet another mountain of scholarly data—toward which he would strike off joyfully. Aghast, the imitative younger scholar had no choice but to follow.

On this occasion that I was remembering in some detail during my trailer recollections, he had been for some minutes rummaging for a reference note. It was one that he had used in one of his published papers about medieval and Renaissance teaching of the *ars disputandi,* or lawyers' arts. He saw the information in the note as being useful for my own emergent term paper on an aspect of William Faulkner's attitude toward women.

I had come to love my mentor dearly, and so I had swallowed my rising laughter that day. Whether I was amused more by the farfetched nature of the connection he saw between medieval pedagogy and the female question, or by the sight of him surrounded by those odd-looking plants, I could not have said. The mental connective was one that would inevitably turn out to be *there.* This much I had learned from previous experiences with what had originally appeared to be random or wild leaps of his mind. And so while my companion scanned and sorted and refiled his slips, I gave myself to some serious reflections concerning the practical consequences of the rigorous scholarly method he practiced.

Now, in my trailer prison, my meandering thoughts paused yet one more time over the mystery of my old teacher. And I found myself turning over some of the same thoughts concerning his scholarly method that I had mulled over on that earlier day and on a number of occasions since. That attitude of his toward research, his evident belief that everything depended upon the care and thoroughness of it—none other among my predominantly Ivy League professors had had anything like my Jesuit's raw passion for knowledge. He was genuinely reverent toward learning.

But at the same time there always seemed to be a curious detachment about him. At times his obvious warm pleasure and heady excitement over ideas even hinted that, with him, learning and proving and disproving comprised some great high game or contest in which he was continually taking his own measure as against something else. Honors did not dampen his enthusiasm. They fell on him like rain over the years—conference chairmanships, honorary degrees, visiting professorships and fellowships in the best U.S. and foreign universities, a decoration by the French Academy—and they marked his personality no more than passing showers mark the earth that routinely absorbs them.

Nor did he seem driven by some need to put down adversaries. In fact, since my teacher was not one to engage in angry polemic and vitriolic criticism, and since he was also curiously nonrevelatory about his inmost feelings toward others, it was difficult even for students and colleagues who were closest to him to decide precisely who or what his true adversaries were.

Ignorance in general, simple lack of information, seemed to be what this driving thinker was most eager to banish from the earth. Hence the legendary lists of required readings, several hundred entries long, which he handed out in all of his classes and kept carefully updated and annotated. Hence his willingness to teach, year after year, long after his seniority could have gotten him relieved of it, one of the English department's "dog" courses, an exhaustive review, for honors and graduate students, of research and bibliographical methods. Hence his working acquaintance with most outstanding foreign and domestic libraries; his enthusiasm for the knowledge explosion; his almost childish excitement over the machine technology that was making the knowledge explosion (and with it, horizon-expanding events like the moon shot) possible. All of these things, it seemed, helped my favorite professor to beat back human darkness.

While I reflected on my old teacher's method of truth-seeking, as part of my melancholy broodings at the guards' post, my thoughts stayed distracted from the gun. Over the years I had never tired of analyzing the distinctive qualities of my loved mentor's mind and method. I could see now, from time's distance, that the very activity that he had been engaged in during the conference that I was remembering, rummaging with endless patience to find a lone notation, was symptomatic of his whole approach. My Jesuit seemed absolutely convinced that somehow, somewhere, every single subject in the world connected to every single other subject. The driving urge of his life in thought seemed to be to tie everything in the world together.

But no. That, I saw, was not exactly right about him either. This first-rate professor of mine had been equally good at dissecting things, pulling them apart, if they did not easily or rightfully belong together. Fixedly I stared at the gun now. But I was not seeing it, so absorbed had I become with satisfactorily pinning down and assessing, this one last time, my mentor's contribution to my life.

He had always had a scathing effect, I remembered, on

superficial analyses of things, and he was especially good at scuttling "pop" explanations of current social phenomena. Were the social scientists or the media telling us solemnly that *this* had given rise to *that*—to pastel-colored appliances and men's dress shirts? to the *Playboy* philosophy? to demands for the vernacular Mass? to the "beat" mode? to the haiku's (or Hemingway's or Elvis Presley's) popularity?

"Well, yes and no," he would comment, or, "After a fashion, perhaps, but . . ." His noes and buts he would always account for with a rapid-fire line-up of at least half a dozen more causes, some immediate and others remote, of the particular phenomenon that was getting so simplistically explained. As well as *this,* he would calmly demonstrate, there was also *this* that surely would have played a part—and this, and this, and this, and this, and very likely this. He could go on as long as his particular audience required. To his own view, obviously, the line of backward-marching and tendril-shooting *this*es continued until it was out of sight, like Gertrude Stein's "rose is a rose is a rose."

Remembering all of this about my inspired teacher, I felt my mind do a kind of squaring off. I grew grimly determined, this being my final hour of life, to crack the essential mystery of how this man's mind worked. I fairly squinted into the time tunnel, as into a microscope, at my old friend.

When I put together his belief in the interconnectedness of all knowledge with his complex notion of causality in time, I discovered that I was able to go further than I ever had before, in my considerations of what made my old teacher tick. What I saw was much simpler than what I expected. He viewed all time, ancient and middle and modern, as being of a piece, with all of its parts interrelated. Applied to scholarship, this meant that the one who set out to gather information, data, about anything, actually had for the parameters of his or her research all the knowledge that had ever been collected about *everything*.

With my discovery that the key to my mentor's mind and personality was his perception of time, I felt another jog to my memory. I remembered the way that our term paper conference of years ago had ended. The note my teacher had been searching for had summarized some philosopher's attitude toward time. Not finding it, but while still peering at slips, he said to me, "The Hopi Indians, you know, don't think of today as a part or section of time, with today next to yesterday, like we do. For them it's always just 'getting later.' " From his tone it seemed as if we had just been talking about Indians. With that he suddenly stood, politely excused himself, and quickly slipped out of the office.

After that, left behind in the empty office, with his overindulged plants yearning toward the scholarly paraphernalia on the desk, I felt my impulse to laugh return with a vengeance. For my part, I cared little whether he found the note or not. I was a part-time student, very casually piling up hours toward a degree. In arranging for the conference, I had been chiefly interested in assuring myself of a good grade on my Faulkner term paper. I had little ambition for saying the last, the definitive, word concerning Faulkner's general attitude toward the female half of the race, let alone pinning down the great author's perception of time.

But I knew that my Jesuit would locate that reference. He always did. If he did not turn it up before I left campus that day, I would very likely find the neatly copied three-by-five slip on the following morning atop my typewriter in my study carrel at the library. It would have been left there by his nocturnal hand. The penmanship would be rounded and beautiful.

A bell rang, and class change noises started up outside. I laughed, a great happy, chuckling whoop of joy that I knew would be drowned out by the commotion outside. I found it thrilling, truly soul-filling, to be a unique and promising young scholar-writer in an outstanding Catholic university at the point in America's history when the Catholic presence, symbolized by Teilhard de Chardin and Pope John and John Kennedy, was being acknowledged everywhere. It was especially exhilarating to have for the director of one's studies the Catholic scholar most at home in the crosscurrents of secular knowledge and the sciences and so most fully attuned to these times. All human problems were ultimately solvable. Of that I was certain. One merely had to lay hold of the pertinent knowledge. And if I personally did not take the trouble to seek that out, my professor would. Or bright university people somewhere would. The future was assured.

At the memory of that triumphant laugh of mine, so long ago in my mentor's office, my trailer thoughts careened to a screeching halt. How idiotic and naïve, I reflected, had been the mind-set that produced that laugh. I winced now to think that I had ever been as ignorant and constitutionally optimistic as I had been on that confident earlier day.

But on the heels of these rueful and embarrassed reflections came a flash of awareness concerning why, in this hour, my thoughts should have turned so long and hard to memories of my old professor. I was right now at the point of winding up the most important research project of my life. I was getting ready to answer, once and for all, Hamlet's searing question: *To be or not to be.* So I had, as never before in my life, to be right. It was natural, I saw, that thoughts of my onetime thesis director should come to mind. By supplying me with as good a method as can be found for becoming well informed, for being *right,* he, more than any other person in my life, had prepared me for this final mile.

Was life worth living or not? It was a subject eminently worthy of research. My mind leaped at it. But then my thoughts suddenly crashed. They had hit solid rock. Why had I not seen it before! My professor's method did not, after all, lead to certainty. It led to *infinity.* Following the lead of this man, who yearned and longed after time, one learned the *last* word on nothing!

Stupefied I sat there over the gun, staring into my past. Childhood, youth, maturity—all were but mountains of *data.* I could sort through their pieces endlessly, I saw, could arrange the data in an infinite variety of constellations, and still not prove anything conclusive. There were always other mountains! Even as I sat there, What-Would-Have-Been rose up in the distance like Everest. I thought I saw truth gleam on its summit before disappearing down its other side. I saw with dismay that even if I died this instant, What-Would-Have-Been would be standing there, generating relevant data.

Feeling almost frenzied now, I threw back my head and laughed. It was an ugly, deep, and ironical laugh. It rebounded dully from the trailer's plastic walls. No wonder I had never discovered the shortcoming in my teacher's inquiry method before. I had never plumbed any subject to its absolute bottom before. I had always discontinued my research at the point where I knew that I had more than enough scholarly ammunition to silence any opposing voices. I had always knowingly left a mountain or two of data unexplored.

My priest-teacher was like a living presence in the trailer now. Out of exasperation with him and the lucidity of mind he had coached into me, I could have beaten on the desk with my fists or kicked its scarred metal drawers. I was betrayed. I had been fired up for truth-seeking, for the accumulation of data, by one who had to have known all the time that to arrive at conclusions solely on the basis of data was to be, in one degree or another, ignorant. About anything, I saw, one generated only partial answers. Even the most compendious research papers were little more than signal flares shot up by mountain climbers who were indicating to fellow search parties just how far and high they had gotten. And the whole rational and positivistic approach to knowledge, I now saw as clear as day, was almost laughably useless when the area of examination was spiritual and religious truth.

I yanked at the edges of the guards' desk, as if to hurl it over. So what was the truth about my life? The only truth that I could see was that there were *two* truths, screamingly contradictory. And I could not prove conclusively which of the two was righter. I could not decide for certain whether my killing myself or my hanging on made the more sense. And the indecision was splitting apart my very brain and being. With a groan I collapsed with my face in my hands, the gun forgotten.

I heard the sergeant's step at the door. He stomped in and buckled up, mumbling about the cold. I, trembling, pretended to be looking over blueprints until he left.

CHAPTER THREE

I tell you solemnly,
anyone who does not welcome
the kingdom of God like a little child
will never enter it.

—Mark 10:15

We are all your children:
'Grant the prayers of your children.'
Amen for ever.

—Pope John XXIII

It was deathly quiet after that. I was exhausted, and there was an odd ringing sound in my ears. For some moments I sat numbly staring, seeing nothing and remembering nothing. When at last I did begin to notice my surroundings, my gradually awakening eye fell on the January 19 *America* that I had buried earlier. Idly, mechanically, I drew it out. Then I sat some moments staring at it dejectedly. What earthly reason was there, I reflected ruefully, for me to keep staying abreast of things?

Largely out of habit, out of a lifetime's intimate association with printed matter, I flipped open the magazine. Feebly, with my mind largely elsewhere, I turned its pages. For some reason my eye was drawn to an article by an unknown woman writer, Patricia Young. This author described very simply how, after a lifetime of nominal Christianity, she had experienced a personal conversion to the Lord and received what she called a baptism in the Holy Spirit at a charismatic prayer meeting in Philadelphia.

A story can compel my attention when most other forms of discourse would not get through to me. Although I was feeling emotionally wrung out and more trapped in my unhappy life than ever, my mind somehow forced its way through this brief piece. I was touched by the openness and the simple, almost simplistic, belief of this magazine writer. But her little piece, faith-filled as it was, stirred me with a great sadness.

How stark was my own soul, compared to this Patricia Young's. What God I had left to me by now was more like a God-shaped blank in the sky, nothing like Patricia's loving Lord and quickening Holy Spirit. I had by this time even grown afraid to pray. The experience had become a terrifying ordeal in which I envisioned the words I spoke as floating aimlessly upward and into space, past the lunar explorations of the 1960s and beyond them into bright blue nothingness. *There was nobody up there listening.*

And yet here was this writer, honest and obviously very intelligent, and publishing in a quality magazine where some of my own work had at one time appeared, who was absolutely certain that she had received an onrush of *something* into her soul as a result of prayer with several persons at a meeting. Despite the nervous exhaustion I was feeling after my latest intellectual crisis, I read her article all the way through a second time.

I decided on impulse to write, then and there, to Patricia Young, care of *America*'s editors. The letter I composed on some sheets I found in the guards' desk could be summarized in one sentence: *How I envy you your faith!* I did not burden this stranger with anything like full details of my spiritual and other miseries, for pride made me loath to reveal how truly desperate I was.

But Patricia Young divined my desperation anyway, for she answered immediately. Her kindly and friendly letter included specific instructions on how I too might "hand my life over to the Lord."

For starters, would you do a small and childlike thing? Soon, when you are alone and you have some time, will you be like a child and just tell Him you want to make one thing clear (to yourself, not Him), namely that you *will*, at that moment, to commit yourself to Jesus Christ. And further, that you acknowledge (to you, not

Him) your absolute inability to work out your
life, and that you literally lay your life at His
feet for Him to take over. And in the conversation will you also give Him your sins to heal?

I was deeply touched. I also felt a slight twinge of
guilt. That I ought to turn to God in childlike faith was
advice that I had been given before. Periodically during
my years of rebellion I had received it from my old Jesuit
teacher, who alone among the priests I knew commanded
my willing respect. Him I had visited intermittently, even
after my graduate studies ended. I had gone to him then
ostensibly for "spiritual direction," but I had come to use
the time of my parlor sessions with my adviser to unbur-
den myself on him concerning the rank unfairness of my
circumstances and those of other married and divorced
Catholics.

Those had been the years when my teacher's fame was
rising, also years when hopes for radical changes in
Church teachings and laws were at their highest. My
friend plainly had access to the thought centers of the
Church. So I told myself, concerning my various griev-
ances, that by burdening my former teacher with them, I
was lodging my complaints "where they would count."

My kindly mentor had, in other words, supplied much
hostility release, and never more than when he counseled
me to childlike faith in God. More than anything else that
he said, this set me to raving.

How could I conceivably be or feel childlike, I would
fume at my priest. Was I not overburdened with being
both parents, fighting my way through life as a solitary
breadwinner, always holding down at least two jobs, cut
off from all of the most basic normal pleasures—from en-
tertainment, creativity, sex, travel, fashions, leisure—ever

buried in children, children's friends, children's teachers, pets, baby-sitters, dayworkers, and all the other freight of children's days. How could I ever be a *childlike* anything. *"Responsibility has beaten all the child out of me!"* This I screamed at my priest one night when I had drunk too much before coming in.

But now here came the urging to childlikeness again. I determined to do what Patricia Young counseled, as foolish as I felt it to be, chiefly because, having initiated this exchange of letters, I felt obliged to her in some way.

It took me some four or five days, my schedule being the way it was, to get "alone and have some time." I had determined also to wait until I felt pretty good physically. In the early morning of January 29, a date that coincided with a birthday in my family, all these things finally came together.

I knelt down beside my bed, an action that reminded me of illustrations I had seen in a children's book about the "Now I Lay Me Down to Sleep" prayer, and I screwed up my courage once again to address words to the God-shaped blank. I prayed in exactly the way that Patricia had advised.

Absolutely nothing happened. There was just my room, the silence, my alarm clock getting ready to ring in the new day. But I felt a bit shaken. I crawled back in bed and sat for some minutes with the covers bunched up around me. I felt nervous, like one who has just stolen something and who hauls up in a quiet place, scarcely breathing, to listen for pursuers.

At length I got up and dressed for work. In my mind I was already seated at the guards' desk late that night, beginning to write to my new friend and to tell her I had carried out her first orders. I planned to ask: Now what? I had in the back of my mind that meantime, until this new thing had played itself out, I would probably not be seriously tempted to suicide. This was too interesting. The writer in me was already growing curious to see how the plot would develop.

While my second letter was taking shape and being posted, my mind kept being teased by one statement Patricia had made in her first letter in answer to some question I had posed to her. "I know," she wrote, "that Our Lord is more greatly pained than you at this long dark night of yours."

That nagged at me. It kept buzzing like a fly around the periphery of my mind. It flew directly in the face of the conviction I firmly held, and had many times thrown angrily up to my long-suffering priest friend, that God and the Church, especially the Church's preposterous laws on birth control and marriage, were direct causes of the wreckage and misery that my adult life had become and of insecurities being inflicted on my children as well. Hence God and the Church, especially the Church, had long been seen by me as causes of my pain, surely not sharers of them.

Having once locked onto this view, I had never once seriously considered that I could be wrong. The case seemed closed. Just as it had been Church law which had overburdened our young marriage, so it was Church law which dictated that I not get a chance at a second start in life. (Things were otherwise with my ex-husband, who had left the Church and remarried.) For me, adult life in the Church had been a struggle in a trap. And in my efforts over the years to pray my way out of my miseries, I had moved only from "There's nobody up there listening" to the even more bitter conviction that "Whoever isn't up there is trying to destroy me."

And yet Patricia Young wrote with authority, as if

there could be no doubt about this, that in my long dark night "Our Lord" was in pain with me. This was a totally fresh view. Unable to get the whole thing to work out logically, I nevertheless wondered whether she could conceivably be onto something. Some long-lost part of me wanted her to be right.

Fright suddenly moved in on me. At some point not long after I took my first weak and unsure steps in faith, I felt panic. Here I was, entirely alone, attempting to lift myself up spiritually by my own ears, as it were, aided only by widely spaced mail communication with a woman I scarcely knew, who was half a continent away.

Haunted by the memory of the struggle with the gun, I felt the need of support closer at hand. My Jesuit professor friend was away for a year on a visiting lectureship, and anyway had shown signs in recent years that there was nothing more he could do for me. No help there.

Nor were there friends. Friends, always a problem for divorcees, had been doubly so for me. I had withdrawn from most academic circles after my recent severe professional reverses had turned me into an object of pity and, in some cases, fear. I had earlier been moved to withdraw from the friendship of most Catholics, finding them either helpless before a set of problems as unique and insoluble as my own or else inclined merely to reinforce my own view that my substantially increasing my income through attainment of the Ph.D. would eliminate some immediate pressures. Meantime they offered small cash loans. Parish circles were virtually closed to me simply because they were naturally uncongenial to bookish females. The complicating factor of my divorced motherhood made the strains, both on me and on the parish group, too much to be borne.

A certain type of Catholic who became very numerous

in the 1960s I had learned to avoid. These were persons
whose own bitterness with the Church, usually over is-
sues of marriage, celibacy, or authority, matched my own.
But unlike me, they seemed to be entirely without the lin-
gering attachment to the old Church and to loved persons
within it that haunted me and made my separation from
the Church, which I had been for years trying to effect,
so excruciating. I knew from experience that my blackest
depressions of all came after time spent with bitter former Catholics.

Faced now with the need for some spiritual support, I
decided, with some misgivings, to take myself to a pentecostal prayer meeting like the one my Philadelphia
friend attended. The only such meeting I knew about in
my city was a regular Saturday night gathering of several
hundred persons at a Catholic girls' academy. I had attended there once, several years before, in the company
of a Catholic lady friend who had been in an exploring
mood.

I had not been impressed. The charismatics struck me
as decidedly odd. The intellectual in me had found the
simple credulity, the childishness, of their individual testimonies about God's activity in their lives to be repul-
sive. Their piety in general seemed connected to nothing
that was familiar to me. It was not pre-Conciliar, a form
of piety which I could no longer practice but for which I
still retained sentimental feelings. Nor was it akin to the
high-minded social activism I had found in the new underground church groups that I had sorted through in my
feverish efforts to find other spiritual moorings.

But for me the most repellent thing about the pentecostal Catholics I had seen on that one occasion had little to
do with piety or doctrine. It related to my having grown
up in a family of German-Irish ancestry, chiefly German,

where the concealment of feelings and repression of emotion were as automatic as breathing.

I could not stand the charismatics' *hugginess*. I who still shrank from the kiss of peace, even when it was a handshake, and who had been doomed by temperament and circumstance to be a loner everywhere, had wanted to flee that setting where even huge men wearing cross or dove pendants embraced each other with bearish eagerness.

But I went back to the Saturday group at the academy anyway. In one sense, I simply had nowhere else to go. What might be called my sense of place drove me to attend a churchy gathering. For despite all my disenchantments and confusions with "the Church," it still remained in my imagination as a distinct place, something you could go to or stay away from. To me one was either really in the Church or really out of it. People's "falling away" from the Church, a process that the embittered friends of mine appeared to have gone through, some with little discernible tearing, had always amazed me. For me, leaving the Church had always involved the definite opening and closing of a door.

Even while preparing, with faint interest, to attend the pentecostal prayer meeting, I viewed myself in relation to the Church as I long had done. I saw myself as just about to exit from the heavy main door of some great Catholic church. My back was turned on what was behind me, including the Blessed Sacrament. I would soon step outside forever, free at last of the machinery of those laws which had made my maturity a prolonged passage through an emotional meat grinder.

But now came this interruption in the form of a tug on my sleeve from my new friend in Philadelphia. In the very act of exiting, I was moved to descend briefly to the church basement, as it were, and to traffic with one more of the many underground groups churning there as a result of the Conciliar reforms.

I decided to take the side trip. For the fact was that the only reason I had been standing for so many years with my hand on the door of the Church of my childhood, with the door partially open, but with me not pushing through it and out, was that I hadn't the faintest idea where, once outside, I would go.

The group was larger than before. All were strangers to me. I huddled among them on my folding chair, one in a large semicircular arrangement of many chairs, all of which faced center. I felt like some stray, a lost dog or sheep, a miserable creature that had dragged in from the cold and whose entrance, fortunately, nobody had noticed.

The hymns they sang were led by some too goody-looking teen-agers who seemed to be under some belief that their being in the Spirit meant they could play guitar without taking lessons. The tunes sounded decidedly Protestant and reminded me of the hymns sung at the church of my little evangelical grandmother, which in fact some of them were. The words were easy to learn, just by singing along.

I joined in, pleased to find that the hymns lent themselves easily to my penchant for singing in natural harmony. The singing helped me to relax a little. I suffered that first night through a rather vapid teaching by a crewcut young priest, John Comer, who was thoroughly convinced that the Father, Son, and Holy Spirit spend their days just pouring down blessings on "the people of God," us. I studied this baby—for men under forty, priests in particular, I had little use—and wondered whether he could be unbalanced. But at the meeting's close, when a woman leader asked those who "had needs" to raise their hands so that the group could pray for them, I remembered what had brought me there and humbly raised mine. I sat with eyes tightly closed then, pleading with the God-shaped blank as I had done before. The strange choric hum of the tongues welled up like a great sea around me as these strange people prayed and I, haltingly, prayed too.

CHAPTER FOUR

Trust is the form grace takes in the poor one who is striving towards God.

—Raïssa Maritain

*A child of God
listens to the words of God;
if you refuse to listen,
it is because you are not God's children.*

—John 8:47

There followed after that night perhaps the strangest several months of my life. Scrambling, as always, to stay ahead of our creditors, I continued the grind of the three jobs. My long, tedious nights in the trailer I passed reading the charismatic books Patricia had recommended: John Sherrill's *They Speak with Other Tongues* (Pyramid), Don Basham's *Face up with a Miracle* (Banner), and Merlin Carothers' *Power in Praise* (Logos).

Carothers' book especially fascinated me. It went a long way toward explaining some of the kinkier aspects of the charismatics' behavior. I learned that the joyful and praiseful spirit that set them as a group so totally at odds with depressed and overtaxed me was not their response to received favors, at least not necessarily. It gradually became clear that the group was praising and thanking the Lord out of pure white-hot faith that blessings and favors *were going to be received*. Theirs was Gospel faith, the faith that Jesus never failed to respond to, the faith that fundamentalists believe can move mountains, can force the hand of the Almighty, as it were, with the weight of Jesus' own promises.

These pentecostals, like all pentecostals, praised and thanked God even before he acted. This practice came through to me as slightly crazy, but in it I recognized elements of the Kierkegaardian "leap of faith" familiar to me from my philosophical studies. That pentecostal beliefs connected in some way to my school studies made me slightly less nervous about them.

Over several weeks' time, the charismatic readings and my exchange of letters with Patricia combined with the

faith-filled meetings on Saturday nights to give my depressed spirits a lift of genuine hope, the first I had
known in many months. But I soon discovered that these
supports to faith were fragile props at best. Two or three
days after every meeting, beaten back down by fatigue, I
would be assailed by all my old doubts and by financial
and other anxieties, and would be bombarded afresh with
a conviction that the friendly charismatics were just a
new kind of religious kook. In fact, every Wednesday or
Thursday would find me wondering whether there was
any point in my continuing to go to the Saturday meetings. But each Saturday I would turn up again, for exactly
the same reason as the first time.

After several weeks of this, even though shyness had
kept me from making friends in the group, I was beginning to feel a bit like a regular. I was moved to ask to be
prayed with privately. Members of the community routinely offered a personalized prayer ministry to persons
who had special needs and who cared to wait around
after the meetings. I was directed to wait in the academy's upstairs chapel, where there were sometimes litur-
gies after the meetings.

There I was approached by a nun in modernized religious dress and a clean-cut young man with a beard.
They asked my name and took me by surprise by inquir-
ing what the problem was. I dared not begin to tell them.
The problem was my whole life. I felt that even to begin
the wretched story would set off such a paroxysm of emotion in me that I would not be able to contain it. I blurted
out, "It's a job problem."

Immediately I realized that for a mistake. They would
of course assume that I was out of a job or had been fired
from a job and would pray for all the wrong things. With
sinking heart I watched them each place a hand on one of

my shoulders, where I sat hunched in a pew, and then lift
their free hands in the charismatic way. The nun prayed
extemporaneously in English, the youth in tongues, and
both of them had their faces raised and their eyes closed.
I was first merely interested, but then stunned by what I
heard.

"Heavenly Father, we come before you in the name of
Jesus, on behalf of our sister Barbara. She is your child,
signed in baptism in the name of the Father, Son, and
Holy Spirit. For her Jesus came, to redeem her from her
sins and to make her evermore worthy of your mercy and
love. Jesus stands with her now, as we do, to remind you
of your promise, given to us by your Divine Son, that
what we ask of you in Jesus' name, we shall absolutely receive. For you do not, would never, give your children
stones, who ask for bread."

The two charismatics continued their prayer. "We be-
seech you now, dearest Heavenly Father, to shower your
mercy and love upon our sad sister by solving this problem with her work. It is keeping her so tired. It is the
source of much confusion and doubt in her own mind,
this awful tiredness. It is putting great strain on her relationships with her children. Heal those relationships, Father, and all of Barbara's other relationships. Break any
bondage she is under from the Evil One. Call her to re-
pent of her sins. Put your healing touch upon her,
Lord Jesus, so that she will come into the fullness of your
life and love. Show her how much you love her, Lord,
and let there be released in her and showered upon her
the power of the Holy Spirit. . . ."

There was more. There were numerous references to
the real and practical problems of my life. This set up in
me such a clamor of astonishment—it was as if this man
and woman had been following me around during my

days—that I heard the last part of their prayer in great distraction.

With the invocation ended, the two assured me that everything was positively going to be all right now. They encouraged me not to flag, now that I had "stepped out in faith." Above all, the young man told me, I must not "look down and get scared." "Keep your eyes on the Lord," he urged. "Keep looking *up*. The Lord has his hand out. Go toward it. Don't look down now, hear?"

I nodded, vaguely stupefied, and they passed on to someone else. I was left alone, reflecting on how true it was, in many senses, that I was now walking "whither I knew not." Before this moment I had sat among these people who claimed to have visions and possess supernatural gifts and had seen nothing that, give and take a bit, I could not account for by the bright clear light of Freud, Jung, Erikson, and others. The prayer of the two pentecostals ended that. So did the immediate aftermath of that prayer. Three days later I was informed by our principal, my chief employer, that with the start of the next school year, because of a severe budget cutback affecting my job and those of two other recently hired teachers, my position was being phased out by the system. In effect, I was to be laid off.

A curious kind of rocking motion came into my life now. At midweek there still came the emotional low, though never so low as before, and with it the conviction that what I was doing on Saturday nights was so weird, so out of character for sensible and well-educated me, that I ought to give it up. I would sit in the gray vault of the trailer and consider how I ought to earn some income on Saturday nights too, instead of wasting time on this religious foolishness. But with the Saturday meeting there would come, just as inevitably, a rising to faith, to real heights of faith sometimes.

And withal, I kept having a feeling that a change was taking place in me, that I was "getting somewhere," as the expression goes. Dared I hope that even the old stuck sled of my life might soon begin to move? Real certainty that something about me was changing came with my re-action to the news of the impending loss of my job. Or-dinarily that news would have thrown me into fits of anxi-ety. Instead, it struck me as funny. So one side of myself, the tenacious rationalist, was amazed to find another, newer side of me emerging, the foolish optimist. When, after a number of weeks, some new friends I made in the prayer group urged me to quit the taxing guard job and to "trust the Lord to pay the bills," I actually did that.

At some point during this curious and prolonged period of "rocking," a disturbing event occurred. In its own way it was to alter my mental outlook as much as the prayer session in the chapel had earlier. It involved a lengthy prophecy given at one of the Saturday night prayer meetings by a slightly plump, bustling woman named Rosemary.

Rosemary looked to be in her early fifties. She attended the meetings alone, and something about her suggested that she was either divorced or a widow. Her manner of dressing always struck me as a bit theatrical and over-done. To the meetings that other women attended in two-piece sport outfits or casual dresses she wore either long gowns or, as on this night, a black velveteen pant suit that had floppy lace cuffs. Her hair was done up youthfully in ringlets and was dyed a bit too rich a brown. She used rouge and the bright red lipsticks that have not been fashionable since the fifties.

So even before this woman's long-winded prophecy

began, a number of things about her appearance had put me on guard. Nor was her personality a kind I find endearing. She was one of those curiously babyfied older women whose breathless and effusive manner, accompanied by blushes and wiggles and nervous pressings of their hands against their bosoms, makes them come across to many persons, cooler women especially, as somewhat artificial.

While a helpful priest was still in the act of adjusting the microphone to her height, Rosemary blurted out that she was absolutely terrified at being up there. She told us how her heart was pounding and her hands were sweating. But she knew very well, she said, that the Lord wanted this particular prophecy to be delivered at this very meeting, tonight. It was an unusually long message, received earlier this week, she explained, a message directed to this prayer community alone, and so—here she lifted a stenographer's notebook—she had written it down word for word, exactly as it had come to her. With that she began to read with quavering voice from the notebook.

The long introduction had made Rosemary's message from the Lord seem to be marked "urgent," and so there was perfect silence as her delivery started. Even children strained forward as if expecting the date of doomsday and more to be revealed in what the Lord had told this very special member of our group.

Taking in all of the woman's prefatory stage-setting, I had grown most uncomfortable. The charismatic gift of prophecy had from the start been perplexing to me. There seemed to be much presumption, even arrogance, in its claims of private revelation. But I had found little to resist in any of the prophecies I had heard so far at these meetings. Once I had gotten over the shock of hearing or-

dinary individuals deliver "God's messages to us" in the
first-person "I," the rest seemed anticlimactic.

The prophetic utterances delivered were rarely original. Most of them sounded as if they had been taken,
with some garbling, directly out of Scripture. So despite
some reservations, as the weeks passed I had gradually
accustomed myself to hearing, from the lips of elderly retirees, wide-hipped nuns, and young mothers with babes
in arms, touching but fairly bland outpourings like, "My
people, my people, I love you. I treasure your thank-
fulness and your praise. You shall always be my people
and I will always be your God." Apart from the Almighty's occasional confusion over when to use "shall"
and "will," nothing in such utterances roused up the skeptic in me.

Not so with Rosemary's rambling effusion. It began
with a solemn announcement that the end times were
upon us and that we were living in the last days right
now. The Good Shepherd was gathering his flock from
the corners of the earth. "I am raising up a mighty army,"
Rosemary cried with feeling, the quaver gone from her
voice. "Come, my lambs, while I lead you into battle with
the Evil One."

The first sharp jolt to me came when the pastoral and
shepherding allusions began to clash with the martial
imagery in riotously mixed metaphors. But then, to make
the rhetorical chaos worse, Rosemary next described some
of the lambs as "skipping over the hills." Now the Blessed
Virgin entered the prophet's vision and started marching,
or perhaps skipping, too. Toward the last, white-robed
angels swung into step behind the Lord, who at some
point had acquired a breastplate of virtue. Mustard seeds,
roses, and "praiseful little chirping birds" somehow attached themselves to this inconceivable army as it moved
"through the hills and valleys."

In other words, breathy Rosemary's urgent prophecy, page after page of it, was consummate drivel. It had been composed by a third-rate mind out of secondhand imagery. Like items of clothing that derelicts put together at Salvation Army stores to make up an outfit, its separate parts were wildly incongruent, clashing.

The literary critic in me had writhed in an agony of embarrassment virtually from the prophecy's opening sentence, and by its close, almost ten minutes later, I was in sweating exhaustion. I was seized by a sudden impulse to flee, now and forever, that basement gathering where such a contemptible utterance as Rosemary's could get by with claiming to be "of the Lord." Had I not been so far up front on this particular night, I would have bolted before the reading ended.

There was a long, heavy silence before the usual ripple of applause thanked the speaker for her contribution. Pink of face, the prophetess minced to her seat. Nervously she fingered the notebook that she carried in front of her as if it were a sacred tome. A young man hurried past her on his way forward to take her place at the microphone, and she gave him a tiny earnest smile.

The youth's voice was excited. "I confirm with my whole heart our sister's marvelous prophecy!" he cried. "Amen here also," called out an older man who in his own haste to get up front was setting the metal chairs clanging.

Bewildered I sat there for the better part of an hour then and watched person after person come forward to confirm or otherwise to relate to the long, ridiculous prophecy. Some witnessed to having recently had a vision exactly like some part of Rosemary's own. Others gave inspired spontaneous teachings, bright little mini-meditations, by drawing upon one or another of the symbols in Rosemary's biblical stew. The battered littérateur in me now found herself unexpectedly faced with astonishing richness of thought. I was actually hard-pressed to take it all in.

In the little meditations, which took off from the prophecy, strikingly original insights abounded. At the point where a young nun took up Rosemary's image, and launched into a thrilling reflection on the Mystical Rose, I began to feel sick at heart that I had no tape recorder along. This was a title of Mary that had long puzzled me. After the nun there came a straw-haired girl of twelve or so whose front teeth were being pressed backward by a long, curving brace that ran around the front of her mouth. The child eagerly confirmed that angels are indeed great strong fighters "for us and the Lord." Liltingly she told of how she would call on her guardian angel regularly to "fight off Satan" and how her angel would leap to the attack.

"My angel wins every time," the gawky young girl insisted. "So now I just say to Satan when he comes around, 'Oh, go away, you old Prince of Garbage, or I'll sic my angel on you.' And Satan goes, *wow*."

By the time the last of the confirming witnesses had concluded, I was close to tears of bafflement and humiliation. The incredible truth was luminously plain: our sister Rosemary's god-awful message from the Lord had struck fire everywhere, like some magical flint. Seeing this, I felt more of my former certitudes collapsing around me, although in my confused state at that moment I could not have said precisely what these were. I knew only that the new and emerging side of me was pointing an accusing finger at the older side of me, the one who devoutly prized her learning and superior esthetic tastes. The dead-serious accuser was saying, "You snob. You vain, hypercritical snob."

CHAPTER FIVE

My dear Wormwood,
Obviously you are making excellent progress.
My only fear is lest in attempting to hurry the patient
you awaken him to a sense of his real position.

—C. S. Lewis

For a week or so after the prophecy incident, I had long arguments with myself concerning the insights that the affair had brought home. The new revelations that had struck down my older assumptions had to do with the relation between art and piety and, closely linked to that relationship, between intelligence and holiness also. If tubby little Rosemary's rhetorical nightmare of a prophecy could inspire, as it certainly had done, profound religious insight and fervent prayer, then could not other forms of tawdry and banal thought and art, through the power of the Spirit, do likewise?

My practice in those peculiar days was to do most of my heavy pondering while driving my car to and from my various jobs, and, with thoughts like these in mind, I soon came to notice in a new way the little plastic Jesuses and Virgin Marys that some drivers had affixed over their dashboards. Previously, I had held these cheap little statuettes to be in the same class as the furry angora dice and gilded baby shoes that other drivers, invariably lower-class types, dangled from their rearview mirrors. But now I clearly recognized the little magnetized statuettes as religious objects. They did not seem class-connected, because they were as likely to be seen on showy late-model Cadillacs as on battered old pickups and family station wagons. They were, like the St. Christopher medals in use by still other drivers, objects not merely decorative but linked to supernatural realities. They were intended to inspire their bearers and wearers to prayer.

Such thoughts of mine, like so many that came to me as a result of the prayer meetings, invariably prompted me to seek for answers by questing back, backwards in time. I recalled my childhood and adolescent selves who had been so spontaneous, so fervent and alive in prayer. Had not my vibrant prayer life in those years been nourished by veritable truckloads of tawdry or sentimental religious objects and writings?

In my mind's eye I sifted through various sacramentals, the kinds of religious articles with which I had had nothing to do for years now: garishly tinted holy cards, glow-in-the-dark statues and pictures, crucifixes whose corpuses had been painted realistically bruised and bloody, lightweight miraculous medals cast out of zinc or tin, Sacred Heart badges and scapulars backed by the cheapest felt.

And then there were the tasteless writings. I winced to recall some of my favorite compositions, ones so well loved then that I had ardently committed parts or all of them to memory: corny mottoes and doggerel poems, overstrained hymns and prayers, saints' lives utterly without verisimilitude, several school lockersful of second- and third-rate religious biographies and novels.

Thinking now about all of my girlhood's aids to prayer, I marveled that I had ever come to "put away the things of a child." The saturation effect of all of that bad art and thought should have been, by all rights, embalming. By the time I was in high school, I reflected half humorously to myself, I had probably owned and lost enough cheap glass rosaries to girdle St. Peter's in Rome and had memorized an awesomely large portion of the Counter-Reformation's grossly didactic bad verse.

These reflections about good and bad art and intellection of course followed me back to the prayer meetings. There they were directly relevant to almost everything I saw and heard during a meeting. The book table, which I learned was invariably a part of charismatic gatherings, was always spread with paperback inspirational works, many of them by famous Protestant evangelists, healers, and missionaries. Catholic academic theologians were in short supply, I noticed, as were Fathers Andrew Greeley and Eugene Kennedy, the *National Catholic Reporter* writers, and other prominent Catholic commentators. Catholic pentecostal writers abounded, though at the time only Fathers Francis MacNutt, O.P., and John Haughey, S.J., were authors known to me. The emphasis in the book selection, apart from the immense popularity of C. S. Lewis, was biblical and devotional rather than theological or scholarly. Bibles were a staple.

A selection of art goods was regularly laid out at one end of the book table. From an artistic standpoint, the items offered ranged from excellent to awful. Handsome Holy Ghost pendants wrought in brushed metal and fired enamel ranged alongside pictures of the "hippie Jesus" and needlepoint Bible covers that made Our Lord look like a cadaver. Clumsy jumbo-sized rosaries called "Jesus beads," which resembled a toddler's educational toy, were hot numbers. Some of the nuns wore them like necklaces. Week after week I shuddered over these necklaces and some bumper stickers on the table that said, "Honk If You Love Jesus."

This community's musicians, meanwhile, did not improve with time. They could take a hymn like "Amazing Grace," which was already set in country-and-western drag time, and make it go so slowly that to slow it down further would have made it go backwards. Some Alleluias, at least at those times when the Spirit appeared to be sleeping, sounded like distant cattle bawling. The effect of them reminded me of a complaint my father always used to make about singing he did not like, that it "sounds like the tune the old cow died on."

Some nights, when the assembly was bawling its Alleluias like old cows, I looked around me at the nuns wearing their flamboyant Jesus beads and the grown men in their cross and dove pendants—the teen-agers preferred *Jesus Lives* buttons—and I felt the same urge to flight as on the night of Rosemary's prophecy. But though I might easily have dropped out, I did not. My self-critical reassessment of some of my own attitudes, which had started on the night of that unpromising prophecy, was having a generally humbling effect.

By now the rocking or alternation pattern, which for some time had seen me swinging between despair and hope, had entered another area. I was aware of zigzagging to and fro, as well, between my old rationalist and modernist habits of mind and my emerging supernaturalism. In my modernist moods I still clung to my old contemptuous attitudes toward dull and boring homilies, gaudy or cheap devotional objects, and anything else religious that was not in intelligent good taste. In the supernaturalist mood I felt a new benign tolerance for the banal and tawdry, and I also found tapping at my brain the old saw to the effect that "God can use ignoble instruments"—invariably Rosemary came to mind—"to do most noble deeds."

Sometimes, close on the heels of that bit of ancient wisdom, there would follow self-probings concerning how my personal tastes, originally nourished on the homespun and sentimental, had gotten so "elevated," so sophisticated. But if I thought very far in that direction, I inevitably found myself overcome by a sweating embarrassment, a feeling very close to guilt.

On the face of things, it would seem that my education had made all the difference, and to some extent it surely had. But my higher education had been gained in Catholic colleges and universities well before the antidevotional and antisupernatural mood of the 1960s had set in every-where. If I had grown coolly rational and sophisticated in my esthetic and religious tastes, that surely had to have less to do with my educational exposures than with some —could it have been?—purely social urge to be like the "best people" of the academic set I moved in after I began teaching.

Many times when I sat among the gentle charismatics, rocking and praising along with them, I grew intensely mindful of what a different breed they were from liberal Catholics of my acquaintance. Status and class consid-erations seemed not to concern the charismatics at all, and so their attitude pointed up sharply the degree to which social considerations affected the actions and atti-tudes of others.

A depressing, half-shocking thought began to hound me sometimes after I had been several hours in the com-pany of charismatics alone. How many once-devout Cath-olics, I wondered, professed religious among them, might have sold out on their faith during the preceding decade or so, out of some venal desire to "keep up with the Joneses," to fit in with the secular humanist temper of our times? Thousands? Hundreds of thousands? It would not have seemed to the slowly defecting ones that this was what was happening to them, I realized, because our minds can trick us where pressures are very subtle. Was not my own mind a perfect example of a self-deceived and biased intellect?

I found myself considering anew what the Media had come to call the "Catholic exodus," that massive rebellion against the Church that I, too, had for years been caught up in. Persons who had joined the exodus invariably artic-ulated its rationale and their own motivations in passion-ately religious terms. But now I asked myself: Might not that mass movement also have been, or maybe even chiefly have been, a stampede by Catholics to be or to seem *upper class?*

Once I had put that troubling question squarely to myself, dozens of examples began to sift in to support my new darkening suspicions. Sometimes while at the prayer meetings, as I mused over the book table with its curious selections of authors, I felt slightly amazed at how imperceptive I had been not to see, long before this, the class implications in the much-touted exodus. It had begun, I saw, long before the Second Vatican Council, which normally received credit for precipitating it. I realized now that even the 1968 furor over the birth control encyclical had been but a surprise twist in a stream already moving swiftly along.

The perfect antitype to the exodus Catholic, I reflected, was writer C. S. Lewis, the adult convert whose books were loved by the charismatics. Writers had in a sense led the exodus. I could think of a large handful of outstanding American writers of this century who had either been raised as Catholics or had early embraced the faith—Ernest Hemingway, F. Scott Fitzgerald, Katherine Anne Porter, James Farrell, Eugene O'Neill, others—but who had "fallen away" as their careers advanced. Before this time my interpretation of these authors' loss of faith, my "reading" of it during my years of graduate study and since, had always been sympathetic to the writers and discrediting to the Church. Obviously, I had told myself, the brighter and more gifted of our intelligentsia were unable, for long, to put up with the foolishly authoritarian Catholic Church, which persists in treating even responsible, mature, and intelligent men and women like children.

But I now saw that the defection of the authors was

open to interpretation in an exactly opposite way. The fact was—and facts, especially long-forgotten ones, were descending on me like rain in those bewildering days—that devout Christian faith and great artistic ability were not only compatible; they had been throughout history the most fertile combination of all.

The faithful and witty C. S. Lewis was at dead center of a great artistic and literary tradition. Even if I discounted Michelangelo and all the Renaissance painters and sculptors and composers, and simply concentrated on literature, I still saw plainly that the greatest richness had been produced by true believers: Dante, Chaucer, Shakespeare, Milton, Donne, Dryden, Johnson, Arnold, Hopkins, and many more. So if, in the last seventy-five years or so, few great artists had appeared in the ranks of devout Christians, that surely announced a defect of our authors more than of the Christian faith. Pretty obviously, when the atheistic and deterministic temper of this age made secularist attitudes a requirement for being *in*—in the smart set, in the mainstream—the gifted writers, like the Catholics of the more recent exodus, shed the embarrassing old faith right quickly.

CHAPTER SIX

> *Deep is calling to deep*
> *as your cataracts roar;*
> *all your waves, your breakers,*
> *have rolled over me.*
>
> —Psalm 42–43:7

> *The religion of God become man*
> *has encountered the religion—for it is a religion—*
> *of man become God.*
>
> —Pope Paul VI, on the New Humanism

> *A bull will butt at red, but you,*
> *Beelzebub, will butt at blue!*
>
> —Leonard Feeney, in a poem on Mary

So went my thoughts during that strange, strange spring. In the month of May the curious rocking period would come to an end. Along with my new friends I would attend the international charismatic conference at Notre Dame University and would be prayed with there for spiritual healing and to receive the baptism of the Holy Spirit. Thereafter, I would be relieved of my cumbersome cart or sled and would be in that state that some have called "flying with the Lord." A better description, perhaps, in terms of the cart or sled such as I saw myself dragging, might be the one given by a charismatic priest friend of mine: "It's like cruising in overdrive."

But Notre Dame and what followed are another story. Here I am writing about praise and, specifically, about the significance to my own life of a very old hymn of praise, "Holy God." Let us get on with that tale.

From the start of the rocking period, which lasted several months, the hymn-singing had worked on me strangely. I gave myself to it more fully from the time that Carothers' book made the attitude behind the hymns, most of which were hymns of praise, more intelligible. But once I did that, I sometimes found myself subject to attacks of emotion so fierce that I feared undergoing them in a public gathering.

Because these pentecostals were mainly Catholics, many of them priests and religious, they alternated the Protestant-sounding Bible hymns with pre-Conciliar Catholic ones. An old Marian or eucharistic hymn would well up spontaneously, joyously, from the group, and, taken by surprise, I would be as if catapulted headlong through the tunnel of time to that enchanted childhood world lit by tree-filtered sunshine and votive candles and the tall white tapers of the Mass. Once again parish May queens and their processions and Forty Hours celebrants preceded by many pairs of choirboys and acolytes wound their stately way through the busy panorama of my God-centered days.

But sometimes during the hymns it seemed as if the sudden motion went the other way, as if something in time's corridor moved out and over me. Sitting there on my folding chair, I would be flooded, virtually overcome, by old sights, sounds, and memories. These washed in on me and over me like a great tidal wave that had originated mysteriously at the far end of my time tunnel and gathered size and force in its churning forward toward today. "Today," of course, remained fixed in my mind as myself in uniform, brooding while at my post in the trailer, earning $2.10 for each hour that passed. Though I had quit that despised job, I still kept in mind, at least in those moments when I lapsed or "blackslid" into my former faithlessness, that I could return to it, if necessary.

The uprushing wave's effect upon me was that of all great friendly waves upon swimmers who breast them in the shallows of some safe beach. I lost my feet, or nearly did, staggered wildly, and finally tipped over completely, riotously. I came up to find myself showered with visions. My eyelashes sparkled. Each pinpoint of light burst into a prism or a star.

One night during especially spirited singing I grew frightened. I was certain that I smelled incense and thought perhaps my good mind had finally started to disassemble from the strains of a lifetime. I began to carry wads of fresh tissues against these strange attacks of emotion during the hymns.

But most of the time my reactions to the singing were not so violent, though they were still extraordinary. The new hymns, the hymns of praise that I was learning, would exert a powerful tranquilizing effect. I first noticed this during successive choruses of the simple, almost puerile, "God Is So Good."

Something would happen, inside me, where the raw nerves usually tensed and strained. There were physical and mental aspects to it. My shoulders would definitely loosen and sag. The effect was akin to the rush of relief brought to the nervous system by alcohol or certain drugs, sensations I knew well. The distresses and anxieties of my days with my teen-age children and my low-paid and unsatisfactory job would begin to seem distant, diminished.

Normally, worry and a chronic sense of impending doom churned around me like smoke from unseen fires. I was ever braced against the worst. But the singing acted like a fresh breeze to blow these frightening clouds away. And when it did so, my hope, like a flower whose head has been beaten into the mud by a storm, would make its first faint struggles to rise.

At these times I would wonder in the depths of myself, "Might not God, after all, truly exist? Might not a loving God be a reality?" And I began to be nagged by the thought that these pentecostal worshipers, for all their oddness, knew a lot of true things that I did not know. For a fact, in proportion as I granted them a few of their premises, their leaders' teachings had seemed to grow in power. I even went so far as to consider how it would change things with me if the charismatics' view of life were objectively right, and mine and that of the secular academic community in general were dead wrong.

Such musings would of course reactivate the old vicious

tug of war. Immediately upon my slightest thought that the pentecostals' view of reality could be an objectively righter, truer, view than my own, the logical and analytical side of me would rise up in howling protest. *"Surely you would not deny your own personal experience!"* While almost simultaneously, under the power of the hymn, there would wind up out of the time tunnel and into my struggling, besieged mind another remark of my Jesuit professor that I had seen fit to jot down in my class notes: *"Experience is not the best teacher."* The inner struggle mounted.

Meantime I began to notice that in the curious mingling and merging of my past and my present, which the time tunnel phenomenon was causing, certain periods of my life were turning out to have more importance than I had attached to them at the time. This was definitely true of my "parish period."

Compared to other stretches of my life that clamored for re-examination, once I had begun attending the charismatic gatherings and rethinking things, the parish period was fairly recent. It had occurred eight or nine years before, while I was still an instructor at the Jesuit school. That put it a couple of years after the divorce, when my long haul toward the doctorate was just gathering impetus, and years before the professional reverses that had so recently undone me in one of our city's public colleges.

The parish period, which was actually just a period of parish activism, had not caused any great turnings in my life. At the time it had simply increased my existing sense of alienation from the Church. So I was surprised to find memories dating from this period coming to haunt me at the prayer meetings and during the days following them. The first recollections came, understandably enough, when the prayer group chanced to sing some of the more

traditional Catholic hymns such as are found in the old
parish hymnals. I was reminded of a miserable experience
I had had, during my stint as an activist, when I had
served as a member of our parish choir. The moment
when my misery peaked had been one in which the old
hymn "Holy God" played a part, and so my reflections
concerning the parish period are important to this present
story.

The time I am calling my parish period had been a
time, the final time, when I had tried to fit myself and my
children into the organized structure of the Church. We
had moved to a new suburban parish, fresh from bad experiences at our former parish where my children had
been taunted by their classmates for being "divorced
Catholics." In the new place we were unknown, and so I
enrolled the children in the school and made up my mind
to become fully active in the new parish.

This experiment was to end miserably, as I have said,
with the hymn "Holy God" playing a part in its most trau-
matic moment, but at the start I found parish affairs en-
gaging. I launched out by attending the newly instituted
and frequent parish assemblies. At these meetings, which
were held in the school cafeteria, some educated Catholic
professional men, mainly teachers and lawyers who
belonged to the parish, were making an effort to bring
what they called the "spirit of Vatican II," which to their
view was a democratic spirit, into parish affairs. Our conservative pastor had reservations about certain aspects of
the laymen's program, but at first he co-operated with
their plans for a parish council and for committees on lit-
urgy, social action, and other aspects of parish life. I, who
had read all of the Council's documents, was impressed
by the sincerity on both sides.

Soon, however, feelings became polarized between the

eager and ambitious laymen and the devout parish "old guard" who rallied around the besieged middle-aged pastor. The bickering and stalemating that ensued eventually caused me to part company from them all, disgustedly calling a plague on both their houses.

When my thoughts at the pentecostal meetings kept returning to this parish period, I had to ask myself why the two experiences were connected, apart from the obvious reminders supplied by the parish-type hymns. The simple explanation soon came. I had been zigzagging or "rocking" during my parish period too, although I had not perceived this very clearly at the time.

The earlier conflict had resulted from the sympathy that I had felt for both of the contending groups, the liberals and the pastor's old guard. And as it turned out, I remained a stranger and sojourner at the parish assemblies, never really settled in and belonged, largely because I failed to settle my ambivalent feelings toward the polarized parish factions, neither one of whose basic attitudes I could fully approve or, for that matter, disapprove. And ironically, thanks to some special circumstances, the tensions between the two mind-sets even followed me to my job, where they beset my lunch hours in particular.

In the Jesuit university where I then held an appointment, the lay faculty group was composed almost entirely of progressive and reform-minded Catholic professionals who, in their respective home parishes, were attempting to do exactly what their liberal counterparts were proposing in my parish. So over the lunch tables in the faculty cafeteria, I found myself listening fairly regularly to amusing or sometimes angry recountings of these teachers' encounters with balky, unregenerate pastors and die-hard ladies of the Rosary Altar Society, the latter of

whom they called "little old ladies with rosaries." In
short, even after I had stopped attending the stormy assemblies in my parish, I found myself forced to sit in at
reruns of events at other parish meetings around town.
The Church's tensions, it seemed, could not be put behind by me.

Meanwhile, back at the parish, my parish, life was continuing. And despite all the heated discussions, it was little changed, as near as I could tell, from parish life the
way it had been since roughly the Council of Trent. Our
stumpy, German-type pastor said the 7 A.M. Mass daily
before a congregation composed of four or five "little old
ladies with rosaries," a policeman on his way home from
night duty, two older couples who appeared to be retirees
—and sometimes me. Server at the Mass was usually a
balding man who had a birth defect and an ungainly
limp, and was one of the parish ushers. At the 8 A.M.
Mass, the parish nuns and schoolchildren swelled these
ranks. Below, in the church basement, once or twice a
month, the parish assemblies continued without me.

Now, sitting among the pentecostal Catholics and recalling these old and discouraging times, I saw clearly the
affinities between the daily Mass crowd at the parish and
the prayerful charismatics. Both groups contained the
prayer people, the supernaturalists, the believers in the
"other world." In hindsight I could see very clearly that
the distance between such supernaturalists and the Catholic academic progressives was immense. Given the progressives' over-all secularism, which showed itself in their
predominantly earthbound vision and their social-science
approach to questions of good and evil, the two groups
subscribed to opposed and perhaps irreconcilable views
of objective reality.

But I also noticed now that my having opted, finally, to

join the ranks of the supernaturalists had not made me
any less uncomfortable in their company. All around me
at the weekly prayer meetings sat what appeared to be
simple devout types, untouched, *pure.* I decided in my
better moments that I might come to like these gentle
folk, but I was certain that I would never become very
much like them. There they would sit, Saturday after Saturday, the "people of God," as they called themselves.
They would sing along, with their eyes gently closed and
their arms raised in prayer. The expressions of them all,
even the very young children, were peacefully ecstatic.

Suddenly one Saturday night, while I was noting all
the detachment around me, I had a long-forgotten memory come bounding to mind. The remembrance involved
an eccentric lady I had known once, a very devout lady
who belonged to the parish choir during the time I have
called my parish period.

My joining the adult choir had been my swan song, my
final attempt at parish involvement. After I had become
soured by the in-fighting between the competing parish
factions, I decided to join the choir. Doing so seemed like
a way to stay involved while avoiding controversy. Also I
had found myself deeply moved by the little choir's singing of certain old familiar hymns at the Sunday Masses.
The songs made me think of happier times and some
loved nuns and priests who had given me my grounding
in Church music. So I took steps to join the small and not
very professional adult group that sang at the later
Masses.

The choir directress welcomed me, and an older lady
who always wore big floppy hats with cabbage roses
around the brim squealed, upon my initial appearance at
choir practice, that surely St. Jude had sent me. This lady
had been praying to St. Jude, saint of the impossible, to

supply the female alto that their little choir desperately needed just then.

Looking back on my choir experience from my place among the charismatics, I could see clearly how my joining the choir might have worked out if my fellow choir members and I had never talked about anything, if we had only sung together, as the Catholic pentecostals and I were doing. But we did converse sometimes. And as I began to discover, with increasing astonishment, how insulated my fellow choir members were from life's harsher realities, from life's realities in general—not to mention the cruel conditions of my own life—I grew panicky to get away from them. These good people were out of touch to a degree that I would not have believed possible in middle-class suburbanites in an age of mass communications. Typical of the choir group were the lady with the big hats, who still called Negroes "darkies," and an older couple who never stopped talking about the pilgrimages that they had made to some European shrines during the preceding summer. The pair owned a vial of Lourdes water.

The choir group, after a few months' time, had driven me into thrashing despair. The members raised up all of my darkest suspicions that God or the fates had marked me out for torments not inflicted on other Christian souls. My actual flight from the choir took place at the close of one Sunday Mass when we were in the act of singing "Holy God." Whenever I was among the choir members, who tended to be "old guard" types, all of the conflicting religious emotions within me tended to rise to the surface. Now, under force of the old hymn, they rose up in a welling crescendo of pain. I could not sing. I wanted to howl, as wounded animals do. So I fled down the winding narrow stairs from the choir loft and out the church's main door to the lot where I had parked my car.

I drove directly home, half blinded by bitter tears, but in my mind I saw myself as speeding away from naïve religious goody-goodies, like those I had met in the choir, and rejoining the group in which (I told myself) I really *belonged,* the university liberals and reformers. Zig and then zag, as usual.

But now here I was, with time having given me better perspective on the two groups between whom I had zigged and zagged so miserably for so long. I could see that with each week that I passed in the company of charismatics, or just thinking like the charismatics, I was choosing the religious conservatives or supernaturalists over the progressives. In my various mental meanderings, both during the meetings and in their aftermath, I was forever making point-to-point comparisons between the two types. Subgroups of the two types came to preoccupy me also.

Sprinkled here and there among the charismatics there were, as well as the nuns in their Jesus beads, other professed religious, most notably some monks and brothers from a nearby monastery and boys' school that was staffed by English Benedictines. Considering the nuns and these monks, men for the most part with superior British educations, I was pained to remember, from years before, some "new nuns" and so-called liberated priests of my acquaintance. In the mid-1960s, these progressive religious had found themselves receiving especially warm acceptance by the brighter and more gifted persons in their respective university circles. As liberal Catholics, they came to be sought out for every faculty cocktail party or professional gathering. Invariably they could be found at these events, surrounded by a knot of interested non-Catholic listeners who, in the spirit of the Kennedy years and just after, were deeply interested in the internal

affairs of the U. S. Catholic Church and in the views of
informed Catholics.

The religious, who were some of the "exodus" Catholics, played the religious-rebel role with great enthusiasm.
To their sympathetic listeners they bad-mouthed, with
equal vehemence, bishops and pastors, Perpetual Help
novenas, the birth-control encyclical, and parish fish fries.
For pink and blue madonnas they had, for some reason,
contempt verging on savagery.

One April night when I could not sleep, I found myself
poring over all of these old memories of academic life.
Why of course, I realized. All of that self-conscious so-
phistication had been a part of the stampede into social
respectability. The dislike of the Virgin Mary was symptomatic, I saw now. Veneration of the Blessed Mother is
considered medieval and old-worldish in academic circles. And no doubt it had at some level reminded the ma-
jority of these rising Catholics of their ethnic origins, their
families' ghetto beginnings in the United States. Perhaps
they felt, not entirely consciously, that in being "above"
Marian devotions they rose higher in the social order.
Had I not had a "Mary problem" myself for many years?
To Mary, virgin and mother, cling in some special way
the flesh and the earth and all lowly things. But these ambitious liberal Catholics that I was remembering had
been frantic to fly.

Now, recalling all of these things as I lay awake thinking, I smiled to consider the monks and others at the pentecostal meetings. Their arms were raised, their eyes were
closed. Liberals they were not, nor swingers either. But
they were flying. Could it be that these, and not the
freedom-talkers, were really free?

CHAPTER SEVEN

The fiend in his own shape is less hideous than when he rages in the breast of man.

— Nathaniel Hawthorne

For new things rise out of the past as surely as old things do. There is nowhere else for them to come from.

— Walter J. Ong

In my love I would give you liberty, confining you only in the Infinite,
I would wall you up in the beauty of God,
In the reach and range of God.

— Charles O'Donnell

Well into April, my intellectual zigzagging continued. At times I felt like a bit of rag someone might tie at the middle of a tug-of-war rope, to show which side is winning. I seemed to be getting jerked back and forth by fiercely warring contenders.

And I could not seem to work out any compromises. The impressions that crowded into my mind as a result of things I heard and saw at the pentecostal meetings, as with those forcing me to choose between the conservative and progressive mind-sets, were not simply at odds with each other. Most often they were opposites. They presented no possibility of resolution, only sharply opposed alternatives, yeses and noes.

From an intellectual standpoint, the situation was a true dilemma. This had not changed appreciably since the time of my broodings in the trailer. I still had two opposed world views to choose between. Either the supernaturalists' view of life was objectively right, or the naturalists' was. Similarly, the Holy Spirit had either inspired the two prayer ministers concerning me, or he had not. Almighty God either had a hand in Rosemary's prophecy and the girl's and others', or he did not. Either the monks at the meetings knew true freedom, or the swinging priests did. And so it went.

Inevitably my feeling of being dragged back and forth by contending forces led me to consider whether actual spiritual powers might be involved. I had of course long ago put aside any belief in evil spirits as real living personalities. In the circles I had previously moved in, such beliefs were unheard of. They were automatically dismissed as "outmoded superstitions." To the secular humanist view, which was generally the academy's, psychology had explained everything that demonology had once believed it accounted for.

But the Bible-oriented charismatics believed unquestioningly in the power of Satan and other evil spirits. To them, evil impulses were not traceable merely to neuroses or to evil-producing societal conditions (though they did not deny the contributions made by these things), but to the agency of consummately evil spiritual intelligences. I had by this time listened to a good number of testimonies at the weekly meetings by persons who claimed to have been freed of this or that "demon of oppression" or "spirit of vice." Some had even named by name the devils—Fear, Self-pity, Envy, Anger, and so forth—whose clutches they had somehow gotten out of.

While stopping short of taking these testifiers for outright liars (I was impressed that they did not look or act like liars), I had all along kept a carefully reserved judgment. I told myself that the ills the religious ones had been cured of had plainly been psychological, and so the curative agent, whatever name they gave to it, had probably been psychological too. The rest I laid to the power of suggestion.

But as my former certainties about other things came to be shaken, so too was my cavalier attitude toward demons. I began to look critically at the knee-jerk reflex by which I had for years handily psychologized most spiritual realities out of existence. That reaction itself now looked to me suspiciously like a psychological defense mechanism.

Might such a reaction not be just another form of biased and prejudicial thinking on my part? I asked myself whether I could honestly say that my own trips to psychologists and psychiatrists for help in solving my religious and other problems had been beneficial.

I definitely could not. Psychiatry had not been able to save my marriage, nor had it appreciably relieved the stresses and anxieties that I personally had borne ever since the divorce. At most a doctor or clinic here and there had supplied drugs to relieve some of the side effects of the more acute pressures—the headaches, jitteriness, insomnia, and so on—but nothing had healed the rawness at the source. Some of the drugs had even produced still more unpleasant or dangerous side effects. So finally, in my own personal experience, psychiatry, which I had once hailed as *the* final solution to human problems of good and evil, had turned out over the long haul to be a very limited science.

Then by what perverse logic, I came to ask myself now, was I continuing to use what I knew of psychiatry's insights and laws in order to discredit the charismatics' testimonials about demons? The self-contradictory character of what I had been doing puzzled and embarrassed me. The witnesses at the meetings, to all appearances sane and happy people, were announcing *cures*—of depressions, of addictions to alcohol and drugs, of neurotic anxieties and fears. So, given my own private experience of the complexity of the psychological, not to mention my also being an anxiety case, why on earth, I began to also ask myself, was I sitting there telling myself concerning the demon talk that all that was "just psychological?" That explanation explained nothing at all.

When the demon question continued to nag me, I went out of my way to obtain and read Reverend Don Basham's fine popular treatment of demonic activity, *Deliver Us from Evil* (Hodder). It answered many of my questions concerning how evil spirits inflict themselves on the body of the faithful, and it called attention to the count-less places where support for Christian belief in devils can be found in Sacred Scripture. Interestingly, nothing in Basham's strongly Protestant book about evil and its agents was at odds with Catholic teaching as I remem-bered it from my Baltimore Catechism days. And at length I found myself moved to consider seriously whether I myself might be, however unwillingly, a victim of Sa-tanic or demonic power.

The strongest influence inclining me toward belief in demons, however, was not my reading. It was the testi-mony of the persons I met during this period of revela-tion, and of one woman especially who became my friend. Ruth was a rawboned person in her middle fifties who came regularly to the Saturday meetings. She first drew my attention because she occasionally would call out her prayerful thanks to the Lord and the Holy Spirit for delivering her from insanity, self-hatred, and a host of other psychological ills, among them "demonic oppres-sion." I found myself growing more and more curious to know this woman's story, but her personality seemed so intense and self-absorbed that my shyness long held me back from approaching her.

Once I did make contact with Ruth, though, I found her to be warm and responsive and in no way reluctant to talk about her psychological history. In fact, I eventually came to think of my friend as a kind of female ancient mariner who had been particularly burdened to tell one story, a death and regeneration narrative, to anyone who would listen.

Ruth was a veteran of two marriages. The first, the Catholic marriage, easily overshadowed my own as a hor-ror story. My friend was mother of six children, then ranging in age from mid-thirties to late teens. Her first husband had been called to service in World War II when he was a young father. He had returned home from the war "angry and with a chip on his shoulder," as Ruth put it. The husband's hostile attitude soon led to his heavy drinking, then to instability on his job, and finally to chaos in the family's financial affairs.

After this there had followed the familiar pattern of domestic strife and financial ruin that I knew from hearing the life histories of other divorced women who had been married to alcoholics. Ruth's husband had eventually deserted his wife and children entirely. The shock of this, combined with all the strain preceding it, precipitated Ruth into a complete mental and emotional breakdown.

My friend related all of this to me over coffee at a restaurant where we went after the meetings. She explained that up until the time of her emotional collapse she had been a routinely practicing Catholic. But total religious despair set in during the course of her therapy. She discovered that she had been placed in the overcrowded state mental hospital in our city. "It was a real snake pit, Barbara," she confided to me, with a shudder over the memory. Ruth had been a depression case, and so electric shock therapy and ice baths were used on her alternately, along with a variety of drugs. Eventually she was presumed to be cured, and so she was allowed to return to her children, whose care had been overseen by relatives of her defecting husband. But Ruth's cure did not last. At any rate, her new stability was insufficient to enable her to cope with the strained family relationships at home, where she attempted a reconciliation with her husband. She was returned to the hospital for another long stay.

It was during this second hospitalization that Ruth had to be told some dreadful news: namely, that her husband was divorcing her in order to remarry and that the children of their marriage were being broken up as a group and distributed to separate charitable agencies. My friend's despair over these events, the humiliation of the one and the piercing grief of the other, made her entirely distraught now. Already in acute depression, she became compulsively suicidal.

"The Evil One had ahold of me, but good," Ruth confided to me, her solitary listener. But then she explained how the taking of one's life in a mental hospital requires a good bit of ingenuity. Since the staff routinely kept sharp and dangerous objects and most cleaning agents out of reach of depressive patients, Ruth was hard pressed to find means of killing herself. But she had no end of time for planning. She saved up her medications and engineered massive overdoses. She pried pieces of sharp metal loose in toilet tanks. She shoved her hands, wet, into live electrical openings.

"But I was a failure in this too, dear," Ruth said with a melancholy smile. "Just like I'd flopped at marriage and motherhood. Which is to say, of course, that Our Dear Lord had other plans for me."

My friend continued the story of her psychological history during our second meeting in the restaurant. For a second time, she said, she was fortunate enough to arrive at a plateau of comparative stability. After she had again been released for some months, and the authorities had become convinced that her second rehabilitation was going to "stick," Ruth was allowed to begin seeking for ways to bring herself and her remaining children (the two older had become self-supporting) under one roof.

This she eventually worked out, but not many months thereafter she entered into a second marriage. In this second union, one she knew was prohibited to her by Church law, Ruth of course had hoped to find the peace and happiness that had been denied to her and the children for so long. But such was not to be. The second marriage, perhaps because from Ruth's side it had been entered into too soon, in a kind of reflex move, lasted less than two years. And it had been during the terrible period after the collapse of this second union, when Ruth was obsessed with thoughts that her mind was again tottering, that a woman friend had invited Ruth to her first prayer meeting.

Ruth told the charismatic part of her story to me during the second coffee session. I should explain here that at the time that I was getting to know this "ancient mariner," she had been "in the Spirit," as charismatics like to put it, for about five years. She knew of my special interest in the demon issue, and so she skipped cursorily over an account of her baptism in the Spirit in order to move her tale along. Like me, Ruth had at first been amazed by the accounts of demonic activity and Christian counter-activity that she heard about at the prayer meetings. But then, she confided to me, she had had all her doubts about the existence of demons dramatically removed as a result of taking part in a deliverance session, a kind of exorcism.

"Gee," I said, deeply impressed, "who was being—delivered?" The word "delivered," which my mind connected with Israel's deliverance from slavery in Egypt, seemed an odd one to use in that context.

"Why me, of course," laughed good-natured Ruth, and she proceeded to tell me the whole strange story. My friend said that during that first year after her baptism in the Spirit, she found, for the first time in her life, the peace of mind and contentment for which she had longed for so many years. She was still subject, at times, to fits of anxiety and depression, ferocious ones, but through all of these she clung to her belief that Jesus, whom she had embraced as Lord of her life, would see her through these dark times. And she had indeed survived them.

So at the end of that first year of her new walk with the Lord, Ruth decided to celebrate prayerfully. She joined other Catholic pentecostals in a charismatic retreat under ecumenical sponsorship at one of our city's lovely retreat houses. There was a healing session scheduled as part of the retreat, and it was at this event that things took an unexpected turning for Ruth.

The minister of healing at the session was the same serious young priest whose teaching on the night of my first prayer meeting had struck me as so optimistic as to be inane. He was leading a small group of the retreatants in prayers of healing for an elderly man, a crippled arthritis victim. While the "laying on of hands" was taking place, the sensitive priest noticed a strong obstruction to the group's prayers, and he stopped the proceedings at once. He looked around at those who were praying with him.

"Has any of you here ever had anything to do with the occult?" the priest asked. My friend gasped in surprise. Years before, during the time when her children had been growing up, she had been badly in need of some kind of diversion from the drudgery of her days. Drawing upon her lifelong interest in writing poetry, Ruth had decided to join a local poetry circle. Not long after she joined them, the members of the poetry group, largely in a spirit of fun, had started to dabble with ouija, and then spiritism. Ruth had joined with her sophisticated friends in these activities and, at least until the poetry circle's doings grew so time-consuming that she had to disaffiliate herself from the group, she shared their interests. Ruth had even attended a couple of seances.

Ruth at first reacted defensively to the suggestion,

raised by the healing minister's question, that she might still be an agent of evil or occult influence. She felt hurt and insulted, for she had been for some time a "born-again Christian," and believed herself to be guided by the Holy Spirit's influence. But the priest explained in kindly fashion that oppression by evil spirits can occur in lives of virtue as well as in lives of vice, as is proved, he said, by the numerous accounts of fierce demonic attacks on saints and other holy persons. As he explained, there needs only to be the right combination of negative and passive circumstances to invite the entry of evil spirits, and it is this perfect combination which spiritism automatically provides. The priest suggested that Ruth might wish to be prayed over for deliverance right there at the retreat. Although the suggestion repelled and frightened Ruth at first, she soon came to see the prudence of it, and so she submitted to what the young minister proposed.

The deliverance session took place later that same evening. The priest called on the prayer support of certain members of the retreat group whom he knew to be experienced in the discernment of spirits or powerful in prayer generally. "It began like any other prayer for healing," my friend told me. "They gathered around me just like they do with somebody who is deaf or has diabetes or a heart condition, and they laid hands on me very gently like they do. Father, of course, first led them in praising the Lord. I remember him specifically praising the Lord for this 'bondage,' as he called it, because through my bondage the Lord's power was going to be revealed anew.

"And then," continued my companion, "Father called upon the holy name of Jesus, and they all did, and now Father said that in Jesus' name they were agreeing together to come against any foul and evil spirits who were

in me or had ever been in me. And then he began to
rebuke those spirits, very authoritative like, with his hand
on my head, calling out at them by names like Self-pity
and Anger and Self-hatred, as if he actually *saw* them.

"My gawd, Barbara," cried my friend, who spoke with
a soft southern drawl, "I felt myself agrowing so *cold*. It
was like my blood was turning to ice. And then there
came this awful grinding noise, like something hard or
brittle was being crushed or broken up. I suddenly realized that this dreadful noise was coming from my own
stomach!"

I gaped at Ruth when she recounted this to me in the
restaurant setting where we were. But meantime I was
scrambling to remember a story once told to me and some
of my friends when we had been teen-agers at the Catholic Youth Center in Peoria. The earlier weird story had
concerned an old woman who had come to the rectory at
St. Mary's Cathedral bothered by "dirty voices in her
stomach."

"Next," said Ruth, "there was this terrible piercing
scream. Which had come out of *me*, of course, though I
didn't know that at the time. And then I started vomiting
up this—gravel and broken glass."

I was horrified. "*Real* broken glass?" I cried.

"Well," considered my companion, "yes and no." She
flung her hands upward in a shrug. "It was real enough
coming up and out, but you couldn't *see* any of it, just
hear the noise of it churning up inside of me." She tossed
a hand as if to indicate that the vomited broken glass was
just as real as the dishes in front of us.

I begged the lady mariner to stop, insisting that I had
heard enough. She leaned forward, concerned, and patted
my hand warmly, to which gesture I gave an answering
pat. "They're all gone now, darlin'," Ruth told me sooth-

ingly. "They got them all. This black lady minister who'd been helping Father with the praying told me the room got so dark at one point that she'd never seen anything like it. And Father John told me how to pray daily against their re-entry, and so my mind is at rest on that score too."

I laughed, a little shakily. "Oh, I know *you're* just fine," I told my new friend. I was remembering her beautiful hope-filled prayers at the weekly meetings. "It's me I'm worried about, silly."

I did find my friend's story distressing, for a couple of reasons. It had of course left me thinking, "There but for the grace of God. . . ." After I had reflected on Ruth's miserable odyssey for a while, I took some measure of comfort from the thought that I had never laid myself open to occult influences in that way, although that avoidance had been entirely by chance on my part. But I was worried when I thought of my bouts with depression and anxiety over the years. These were states of mind very like some of those she had described.

But after I had taken all of the worrisome things into account, there was one thing in particular in my life that stood out as looking very much like the work of some evil power or powers. This was the strange mental darkness, a kind of predisposition of my intelligence, which, until just recently when I had begun taking critical note of certain biased habits of my mind, had caused me to block out certain understandings and to fix or lock on certain others.

The total effect of this biased thinking was negative. Its end results had been prolonged rebellion against the Church and, for my own psyche, hopelessness and despair. For the strange darkness had not only given birth to a number of key untruths and erring mental habits, of which my psychological-mindedness was one, but it had ensured that any contrary evidence, like facts that could have unseated my wrong notions, had never penetrated my consciousness at all.

The chief mysterious blind spot that I had long had, the one that to me looked most suspicious, however, was not my automatic reliance on pop psychological explanations, as foolish as that practice had been. It was my certain conviction, unshaken over many years now, that what had chiefly destroyed my marriage was the effect upon it of the Church's stringent laws against family planning. Driving home from a prayer meeting one night, I found myself appalled to reflect on how hastily I had snatched up that explanation for an event as complex and prolonged as the collapse of a marriage.

This view was a "reading" that I had given to my life years before, and then, with about as much discernment as a mud turtle with jaws clamped blindly on a stick, had held on to fiercely ever since. Why, I now wondered, had it never occurred to me, the presumably cool and rational woman of thought, that from earliest times in the Church, Christian marriages far more disadvantaged than mine had somehow been surviving.

Had I not just recently sat at prayer meetings alongside the apparently happy children of some Catholic policeman or insurance salesman who was supporting perhaps five to eleven children? The guardian-angel girl was herself from a supermarket manager's family of tow-headed youngsters whose number, because they all looked alike, I had not yet managed to establish.

Mulling over my closed-mindedness, I found it insufferably ironic that over the past ten years or more I had continued to think of myself as a clear-headed rationalist and something of a scholar. I squirmed a bit to reflect that I even had a small reputation as an unbiased literary critic. My literary peers on occasion had observed of me approvingly that I was one of those critics without axes to grind. I approached novels and plays with my mind open to multiple interpretations or readings of them, and I always encouraged my students to do the same. Then how, I asked myself, had I come to start behaving like a mud turtle in relation to the data of my own life history?

The name "Prince of Darkness" began to have a special meaning for me. Conceivably, might an evil intelligence have been working all along to ensure that my "right mind" never should notice what my "left mind" was doing? Could my naturally keen and questing intelligence deliberately have been kept in the dark, so that untruth and rebellion would reign unopposed over my mind and heart?

Such questions now entered my consciousness with the force of small explosions. As each new one struck home, I felt more put upon by warring contenders than ever, which only increased my curious apprehension of myself as a battleground. A kind of fear began to stalk my thoughts now. If I had been so out of control all along, when I had been so certain that I was being clear-sighted and realistic, wherever was I now, with so many uncertainties crowding in? And ought I to continue this painful odyssey into self-knowledge? To what or where was it leading, I wondered.

Again I felt a two-way pull. The passionate truth-seeker in me longed to press on. But another part of me was growing frightened. Every rock I had turned over thus far had had something live and wriggling underneath. How many more scorpions were on my desert's floor?

And of course, at the same time that I had been wrestling with the question of demons, I had continued to receive jolts of one kind and another from events at the prayer meetings. Definitely one of the most fascinating things about the pentecostal Catholics, with whom I had been taking my uncertain steps into faith, was their belief in the presence of the Lord at their meetings. They took with perfect literalness the Lord's promise to be "in the midst" whenever two or three were gathered together in his name.

To be sure, the Church has always taught this about the Lord's presence in gatherings of believers, and Catholics have always believed it. But I do not think that Catholics have always believed it the way these charismatic Catholics believe it. They do not just believe and know the Lord to be with them. They experience his presence. It would not be wrong to say that this group *saw* the Lord in their assembly.

Discovering this about the charismatics had at first faintly scandalized me. It smacked of some Protestants' offensive chumminess with the (I was used to calling him "Our") Lord, their he-walks-with-me-talks-with-me attitude toward Jesus. I was one who, even in my prayerless years, had thrilled to the notion of the Cosmic Christ presented to me through my hungry readings and rereadings of Teilhard de Chardin. I wanted no part of any folksy, lower-class Jesus.

But the skeptic in me currently found herself fighting to keep her feet. Each week I had sat among people—ordinary and sane-looking married couples and professed religious and long-haired teen-agers and incredibly rapt and attentive children and toddlers—who *talked* to the Jesus in our midst. They would invoke and pray and praise and then, with shining faces whose perfect joyousness always startled me, would call out with love to Jesus' ghostly presence.

There was no way, I realized, nor was there even any

reason, for the Jesus phenomenon to be a mass put-on. Nor could I make any theory about mass hysteria stick. The thing happened regularly, almost casually, each week, and it began soon after people had first sat down and removed their wraps.

"Spirit of the living God, fall afresh on us. . . ." They would always include this hymn near the start. Then they would move on to another especially gentle one like "Father, We Adore You," which they knew how to do as a stirring round. Every once in a while (amazingly, since this was long after Christmas) they would break into "O Come Let Us Adore Him."

Then it would happen—the emergence of the Lord. I began to know the precise moment because of the sense of awe and the rash of goose bumps that passed over me. Once when the Spirit-filled Dominican, Father Francis MacNutt, conducted a healing service in the packed upstairs chapel, he described the healing Lord as moving among us in the manner in which he did at the Last Supper, with towel and basin in hand. MacNutt told us that indeed the Lord was passing from one to another of those who had prayed for healings. "He is moving backwards in time also, to heal those painful memories."

I too began that night, at least in my mind's eye, to see the Lord ministering to us lovingly. His familiar face and form from a hundred paintings, statues, school texts, holy cards, medals, stained-glass windows, vestments, and magazine and calendar covers flowed around me eerily, as if in a timeless pageant. He was the same "Our Lord" whom I had encountered and recognized on my childhood's secret pathways along the creeks and hills. As then, his hands were wounded.

CHAPTER EIGHT

He fathers-forth whose beauty is past change:
Praise him.

—Gerard Manley Hopkins

Nothing now exists but himself, this shell, and the
storm. The windows clatter; the sand has turned
to gravel, the rain has turned to sleet. The storm
seizes the church by its steeple and shakes, but the
walls were built with love, and withstand.

—John Updike

At these times when the Spirit seemed to be moving everywhere, when the Lord seemed most real and touchable, I knew beyond any doubt that I was getting somewhere, that I was really moving, in my journey into faith. But sadly for me, the contact with Our Lord and the Holy Spirit was not primarily what was needed. It was the reality of the loving Father that my life history had denied.

In most women there seems to be a need that is interwoven with those for food and warmth and sex and love, the basic needs, though it is clearly distinct from them. This is the need to be provided for by others, family in general, but most properly by fathers, husbands, or lovers. I had known, long before my charismatic involvement occurred, that the God-shaped blank in my heavens looked suspiciously like the generous personal provider that I had not had since my early childhood. This was when the sudden onset of World War II, when I was nine, had wiped out my father's source of livelihood and, with it, his loving spirit, and had made heavy work and cash earnings necessities for even the youngest children in my family. In greater and lesser degree, increasingly greater, I had been forced to make my own uncertain way since.

Now, the spirits or fates who guide our judgments are not discriminating intelligences. Or more likely, it is we who fail to make important distinctions when they have us in their power. Either way, it had not seemed to make any appreciable difference to my psyche that life's goods, comforts, and securities had not been withheld from me, either in childhood or maturity, through anybody's malice. In the economy of evil, a father's bad luck and a young husband's weakness will do nicely, thank you, to make the universe an overwhelming and terrifying place. And so they had.

By this time my contact with Patricia Young and with the pentecostal Catholics of my own city, as well as the charismatic books I was reading, had sharpened my interest in Sacred Scripture. And as I read the Bible, references to the Father riveted my attention especially. At least they did so, once I had fallen into the charismatics' practice (also one of their premises) of accepting everything in the Bible as revealed truth. I frequently mulled over Jesus' most revealing statements about his relationship with the Father and our own relationship with the Father. These were texts like "I and my Father are one" (John 10:30), "No man cometh to the Father except by me" (John 14:6), and "No man can come unto me, except it were given unto him by my Father" (John 6:65). My meditations on the Bible left me with the disturbing impression that to make contact with the Father was both utterly simple and bafflingly complex.

During the period that I was most taken up by these thoughts about the Father, roughly the Easter season and after, my mind for some reason kept returning to those years when I had intermittently visited my Jesuit literary mentor to avail myself of spiritual guidance, hostility release, and a number of other benefits that his friendship afforded me.

My teacher had seemed to take a special interest in my happiness during the years when he had been my graduate professor. And at the somewhat later time that I began to consult him about my personal problems, I had been painfully aware that a need to feel almost complete dependence on my kindly adviser was what chiefly sent me back to him again and again. During our conferences

over spiritual matters, I had even caught myself sometimes being testier and more insolent with my old professor than I actually felt, this apparently out of some recurrent need to try the strength of his affection for me.
Would he love me even if I were difficult—sulky, defiant,
and ungrateful? I had to know.

During the period that I was consulting my Jesuit
friend on matters of faith, it had been a source of embarrassment to me that this acclaimed scholar, who was
reputed to know more about human thinking and behavior than many psychiatrists do, knew about these psychic
needs of mine. But he never made any reference, either in
our conferences or at other times, to how much he perceived about my needs, and so he spared my tempestuous
pride. He always dealt very seriously with the intellectual
and spiritual difficulties that I brought up across the conference table. He acted as if these were indeed my pri-
mary and only reasons for coming in.

With my new realization, thanks to the charismatic
influences, that my doubts about God's existence rose
from my almost blanket disbelief in Divine Providence, in
the Father Creator's continued caring, I felt a new rush of
fondness for and gratitude to my old teacher. How much,
I wondered retrospectively, had his living presence done
for all those years to fill in, temporarily at least, the
father-shaped blank in my black, black sky.

My periodic parlor conferences with my spiritual director had of course been interspersed with occasional
purely academic conferences in his office, meetings simi-
lar to the one I have already described. But in my mind,
and I believe in my adviser's mind too, these routine conferences about manuscripts and other research matters
were entirely separate from the more spiritual conferences. The latter were even held in a different setting, the

formal parlors near the cloister where the Jesuits regularly saw visitors. The spiritual conferences continued for
almost ten years and would have involved upward of
twenty-five or thirty different meetings, all aimed at rec-
onciling me with the Church or easing some of my problems of faith. In undertaking to assist the problems of my
soul, my priest had two things chiefly in his favor. These
were my unrelenting affection for him personally and my
abiding respect for the power of his mind. He remained
the only man alive whose philosophical and psychological
judgments I considered fully informed and therefore basically sound.

Brooding over my felt need now to come to some living
relationship with God the Father, I found my thoughts
returning almost obsessively to one parlor conference in
particular that I had had with my priest. This memorable
session had peaked in an explosive exchange between my
adviser and me. And what my old friend and I had
clashed about on that night bore directly on the problem
that concerned me now: namely, my need to establish
contact with the Father.

In my meandering memories in this strange spring, the
singular parlor scene from years before kept coming back,
as alive and fresh as morning. I found myself repeatedly
going over its details. The session had started in the usual,
almost ritual, way of all of our parlor talks. I waited as I
had so many times before, seated on one side of a big
square antique dining table in one of the high-ceilinged
old parlors near the Jesuits' chapel. This parlor was in the
university's big old administration building. As soon as
the clock in the soaring tower of the medieval Gothic
church next door bonged 8 P.M., I knew that I would hear
my friend's footfall in exactly one minute, at most two.
His pause in the corridor outside would be to tell the op-

erator at the telephone switchboard to hold his calls. His punctuality, like his perfect courtesy, never failed.

Hearing that familiar tread, I always felt a small wave of amazement. He had come—again. As I have already intimated, for all practical purposes, at least from my side, many of my conferences with this high-domed, thin-haired churchman of middle age might have ended there, with his simple arrival at the opposite side of that old black-varnished table. My feeling was that in the case of the spiritual conferences he had no obligation to see me, such as he did have in his role as one of my graduate professors. And it is surely a sign that I held my own company in generally low esteem that I lived in continual dread of his turning down my requests to talk to him about the matters of my soul.

After my student days were over, the mere logistics of the situation would have seemed to call for a polite brush-off. I knew from my student days what my mentor's teaching and academic counseling schedule was like, and I could guess at the number of mail and phone communications, not to mention all the faculty business and graduate oral examinations, that consumed his days besides. Too, I had early recognized in this voluminous author a compulsive creative writer such as I myself was, a driven person for whom every free moment had to be precious. So the more honors that had come to be heaped upon my priest with the passing years, the more fearfully I braced myself against rejection. It never came.

On the particular night that my Jesuit and I were to reach a crashing impasse, it was snowing. During the minute and a half between the old clock's bonging and my director's footsteps at the door, I had been brooding at the parlor window. I was peering through the slats in the dusty venetian blinds at the soft heavy snow coming down in a street-lighted intersection half a block away. So too, I was reflecting gloomily, had I waited for this faithful and tireless man on nights when the parlor was so hot that neither the whining of mosquitoes against the dusty old screens nor the clanging of the passing streetcars cut very far into the dead mass of heat in the room. So too in the autumns when undergraduates flipped footballs and Frisbees back and forth on the patch of lawn one story below. So too in the springs. Then the bridal wreath bushes surged up like fountains below this window.

I heard him step into the room. He was always somewhat formal at the start. "Good evening, Barbara," he said now. He was standing beside the chair on his side until I should be seated on mine. He was in his cassock, as he most often was. If he was braced for displays of unpleasantness from me this night, he gave no sign. As on all other occasions he was pleasant, earnest, open, expectant, and he seemed glad to see me. I knew that our conversation would go exactly where I chose to take it. It was always that way.

When he had sat down, I shoved across the table at him a dark heavy volume that I had brought in with me. This was Louis Bouyer's *History of Christian Spirituality*. "I couldn't hack the Bouyer, Father. You can have it back. I believe it's checked out in your name."

He frowned, plainly puzzled. "What's wrong? It's just straight exposition." I hedged. I was mildly annoyed at having to admit, to my comparatively low-keyed friend, that when certain subjects were involved, even the blandest discursive prose could send me into fits of exasperation.

"Oh, I know," I tossed off. "The first half, the historical background on the Old and New Testaments especially, was rich. I'm glad you gave it to me," I added, out of concern for his feelings. "It put things together. Like you said it would. But when he got into those devotions . . ." I made a face.

"What?" He still looked puzzled.

"Devotions. *Devotions*," I said irritably. "The rosary. All those medieval practices. The whole Mary thing. I had to give it up."

"Oh," he said. He looked a bit crestfallen. But he nodded, as if he might have dimly understood why I had found the "Mary thing" hard to take.

"Father, those beliefs are so *fantastical*. Surely you didn't expect me to grant them any credence, albeit they have their place in Bouyer's treatment."

When he didn't assent to my point at once, but just sat there blinking off into the distance and getting ready to say something, I pressed on. "My God, Father! The Middle Ages are nice to read about in Curtius, and you've even interested me in commonplace books and dialectics and oral residue and— But I mean, surely you don't want us"—I pretended to speak for all of his students—"to begin *thinking* like the medievals."

"Ye-es," he said uncertainly, "*fantastical* in one of its senses."

Discovering him to be still etymologizing "fantastical," I felt annoyed. I hurried to put as many barricading thoughts as possible between his whip-smart mind and me. "I mean, relics, *pilgrimages*, for God's sake. What was Bouyer saving for his last chapter—Lourdes water? I was afraid to look."

At this point I discovered with slight surprise that already tonight we had reached the confrontation point that usually we did not come to until after the half hour had struck in the tower above. This was that painful crisis time—had he learned to dread it too, I wondered—when my half-crazed unbelief stared across the table at his quiet faith and could not believe, no, could not cope with, could not *stand* what it saw.

There was something terrible about the faith of my reserved and studious spiritual director. I always felt personally, almost violently, assaulted by it. The basic irony touching him and me was so comprehensive that it made me feel breathless, giddy. By far the strongest nourishment that had been given to my urges to independent and critical thought, which because of my circumstances I had turned violently against God and the Church, had come from books on *his* class reading lists during the late fifties: Teilhard de Chardin, Mircea Eliade, Sartre and Camus and all of the existentialist philosophers and novelists, Freud, Jung, and Erikson, McLuhan and a number of other communications theorists, Moltmann and other "demythologizing" theologians, William James and the modern pragmatists and logical positivists, and great secular humanists like Fromm and Buber. And then there had been those mental habits learned from him, the alertness to shallow thinking and unexamined assumptions, the eagerness to rethink *everything*.

I knew that my great teacher knew all that was in these authors' exciting books and knew much, much more besides. Some scholar-critics had even called his "the last encyclopedic mind." And so his continuing to think and feel the way that he did about God and the Church was totally incomprehensible to me. There seemed some outrage in it.

That night I felt some crazy impulse to try to traverse the abyss that lay between us. Perhaps I could bargain with him. I lifted a negotiating finger. "Look, Father," I said, "I know you wouldn't lie to me about anything, right?" With dismay I saw that my finger was shaking.

He looked up, his face open, hopeful. "No, no, of course not, Barbara," he said earnestly. His expression still carried traces of puzzlement and, now, at my manner, a hint of mild alarm.

"I believe you," I told him. "I don't think you ever have lied to me. Not about anything. Not even through all the thirty-three revisions of my old Joyce thesis," I added, with a lame attempt at humor. "So, Father, tell me—"

Having come that far, I grew afraid to forge on. It seemed as if I might trigger something terrible. "Do you still—I mean—well, do you—*say the rosary?*" I was shocked at how hoarse my question sounded. Mine was the voice of one terrified.

He blinked once and looked surprised. "Why, yes of course. I say it every day. I used to try to say all three—"

"*Oh!*" I leaped to my feet, looking at him wildly. "Father, you can't possibly. I mean, you can't possibly really believe—"

I could not summon rationally what I was trying to say. It churned up inside of me like some malignant mass. I felt overcome, as on the Sunday when I had fled from Mass in terrible distress over the singing of "Holy God." I thought compassionately of animals that throw back their heads and bay at the moon, get it out.

Discovering myself on my feet then, I was torn in opposite directions. I longed to rush around the table and fling myself on my knees before my companion. I would cry to him, *"Please, oh, please, Father. Give me your faith!"* I would grab him around the middle and shake the trunk of him until heaven fell on me at last and I could sob my miserable life away in his lap. Standing there, I could almost feel the cassock's coarse black serge against my face.

But instead I composed and steadied myself. "Father,

how *can* you pray the rosary?" I demanded coolly. Meantime my Ivan Karamazov mood was still on me and my thoughts raged and whirled confusedly. Freedom, responsibility, commitment, choice—snippets of existentialist rhetoric buzzed like hornets through my brain. *How could he still believe!*

But he interrupted. "Naw, naw, now, Barbara, come on." He swept his left hand up, as if motioning a puppy or a child into his lap, and flipped his cincture across his knees with his right. "You're getting all excited over nothing, now," he added, smiling softly.

"It is *not* nothing," I told him huffily. Privately I was hoping he would never use that midwestern *naw, naw* before the pundits of the Modern Language Association. They might pounce on it, the way some reviewers had pounced on the faith touches in his books, for a sign that the religious mind is basically flawed, lacks class.

"Yes it is," he insisted. He had swung his knees straight under the table. "C'mon now. Sit back down," he ordered gently. He was smiling fondly over at me. My cheeks felt hot, burning. Muttering, I finally sat back down.

Then, without asking any leave from me, the amazing man across the table began to talk just as fondly and familiarly of Our Lord and Our Lady and the "old Church," as he called her.

I slumped then. This had happened before, his taking off this way. Feeling wrecked and curiously beaten, I sat dully staring at some spot across the room, scarcely listening to him. I was overwhelmed by the unreality of it all, as I had been every other time this happened. He had ways of tying his meandering spiritual and scholarly reflections to old literary papers of mine and to incidental things that I had told him about my children. People he knew got pulled into these little spiritual monologues. Tonight I heard mention of Margaret Mead and Père Jean Danielou and his own mother. These would get scrambled in among persons whom he and I both knew, or knew of, like the university's rare-book librarian and Walter Cronkite and St. Monica and Shakespeare's Bottom and old Father McAddie, who tended the campus petunia beds.

But this night he eventually said something that forced my numbed brain to stir. "So you see, Barbara, you really must pray." His voice was deeply serious. "No matter how hard it is for you. You really must do that now." He sounded almost singsongy and lyrical at the last, as if he might have rehearsed this part before coming in.

My exasperation started up. "Oh, God." I moaned aloud and rolled my eyes skyward. "Here he comes again. The hurrying feet." In my imagination I saw my Jesuit loping relentlessly on, like some old flop-eared hound, the hound of heaven from Thompson's poem. I was the dumb rabbit bounding wildly up ahead. "Lippity lippity, through the fields of florilegia," I muttered aloud, mainly to myself.

He heard it. "No, I mean that, now," he insisted. He rubbed the sleeve of his cassock briskly back and forth on the table's surface, at work on some spot or stain. His voice carried an edge of annoyance. He had obviously read my mind concerning his tenacity as a hound of heaven and had caught the chase imagery and the sarcasm.

"Father," I snapped, "you know very well I can't pray."

"Yes you can," he shot back. He seemed ready to fight. This was something different.

"I can *not*. How can I possibly pray when I know very well there's nobody up there listening?" I sniffed derisively. "Lord, I shouldn't have to be telling *you*, a world-famous communications theorist, that."

"Then you pray anyway." It sounded distinctly like an order.

I drew up, roused. "Father," I fairly squealed, "why on *earth* should I pray under those conditions? Why? Tell me that. *Why?*"

In reply he slammed his palm down on the table to make a smacking wham. The sudden blow sent a light metal ashtray spinning sideways off the table and rattled the old windows. "*Because Our Lord said so, that's why!*"

Stunned, I stared at him. I had never seen him like this before. His eyes blazed behind his glasses. For a long moment we two faced each other, faces open and exposed, frozen in the confrontation. I was the first to back down, although I was still too stunned by his unprecedented display of force to say anything. I heard him clear his throat in the little room that was still ringing from his blow on the table. He had retrieved the ashtray. His voice sounded hoarse and tired, and I could tell that he was embarrassed by his anger.

"Our Lord said we must pray," he urged softly. "Always, Barbara. To the Father. And he even gave us the exact words we must use. The 'Our Father.' Here, now. You say it after me: *Our Father who art in heaven*. . . . Come on, now. . . ."

I tried, but no words came. My throat had closed with my need to cry. I was in acute pain, longing again to lay my head in his sheltering loving lap and bawl away the years.

"*Who art in heaven . . . Hallowed be Thy name; . . . Thy kingdom come. . . .*" I let him finish it alone, although I managed a hoarse amen. We both stood then, together sensing that another of these futile conferences was over.

"Thank you, Father," I told him sincerely as I went out. He caught up with me in the dim corridor after turning out the lights in the conference room, and then he made pointless small talk about the snow as we walked together to the main front door of the old university building. The clock in the church tower was bonging the quarter hour after nine.

We two exited the building under a stone archway that was half a story above ground level, and he watched from the top of the steps while I descended to the sidewalk and plowed my way toward my car parked along the street half a block away. I turned once to see him still standing up there, his loved black form hazy with snow. He was hunching his slight frame against the wind as the cassock billowed out. I waved to him weakly. He lifted his right hand once and disappeared.

Recalling that night now, so many years later, a night that I had returned to in memory many times before, I found that its elusive core, its mystery, still partly escaped me. I turned his formulation over in my mind: *Do it because Our Lord told you to.* I saw now how he shared with the charismatics that childlike reverence for the revelatory truth of the Bible.

But I well knew what construction progressive Catholic friends of mine would place on that attitude of his toward biblical directives. I thought especially of one brilliant girl friend who had by now fallen away. They would laugh at it. "Oh sure," they would sneer, "that is just like the Church. And that would be just like him," they would add, "the 'Jesuits' Jesuit,' to put it that way: Do it because authority says so. And *wham*, that's that."

But now that I looked back on that long-ago snowy night and reconsidered my good priest's thunderous order to me, was there not something to be said for his view? Might there not be a great deal of wisdom in it? If God really was somehow our loving parent, would not laws, direct orders from him, including prescriptions for us that were given by his son, Jesus, be entirely in order? Even human parents, I reflected, commonly know far more than their children do about what is good for those children. And with what grief do most parents have to watch their children endangering or diminishing or defeating themselves by defying the directives of those who will for them only happiness.

I thought back to numerous incidents with my own children. First as babies, "Oh! Honey, *don't* put the old dead moth in the mouth. *Ooh. Ick. Yikky.*" And in the school years, "No, now, boys, don't ride those bikes in the street after dark. It's dangerous. Absolutely not. That's that." And most recently, "Girls, dears, *please* don't start smoking. It's expensive. It's addictive. You'll just have to kick it like I did. Don't, now. Don't."

To all of which, when babies and teen-agers alike, my children had often responded with their who-does-she-think-she-is look—as they trotted off to play on some expressway. Their bolder way was sometimes to whine, "Aw gee, Mom, why do we always have to do everything *your* way?"

My loving heart had broken many times under their silly defiances. And thinking now about my exceptionally good children and me, I felt a sudden rush of insight into what it might feel like to be God the Father of the human race. This was one more of those revelatory flashes that in those days were striking me like explosions. It had come on during the pentecostals' quiet singing one night of "Father, We Adore You."

As if clouds had suddenly parted, I imagined that I saw the Heavenly Father, yearning out over Teilhardian cosmic space, hovering over the race in its infancy. "Do not eat of the tree of good and evil." *Yikky*. Do not touch

dead bodies. . . . Burn houses where leprosy has
thrived. . . . Do not eat blood meat." *Dangerous*. And I
saw Jesus instructing those he loved, "Pray like this: Our
Father who art in heaven. . . ." *Follow me*.

Now my researchings of the Scriptures, John's gospel
especially, came to fill my God-starved, Father-hungry
heart to overflowing. So eager was I to catch nuances that
I compared different biblical translations. This was what
I was doing in the middle of one night when, for some
reason, I had waked up fresh and rested and with my
thoughts burning on God. A text from the Jerusalem
Bible leaped from the page:

Do you know why you cannot take in what I say? It is
   because
you are unable to understand my language.
The devil is your father,
and you prefer to do
what your father wants.

                                        —John 8:43–44

"No!" I cried, bent over the living page. "*No!*" I got out
of bed and fell to my knees. An immense pity came over
me as I thought of the heartbreak of the Father. I began
to pray with arms raised, in the charismatic way. "O poor
dear Father," I whispered with anguish into the darkness
surrounding me. I felt hot tears coming, and I knew that I
would approach one of the parish priests soon and par-
take of the sacrament of Penance whose meaning had
been hidden from me for years. "*O my God, I am heartily
sorry for having offended Thee. And I detest all my
sins. . . .*"

I followed my soulful Act of Contrition with an Our

Father whispered from the deepest reaches of my soul. *"Our Father who art in heaven. . . ."* Again I saw the snow hazing my director's loved black form in the archway above, and I saw him raise his hand.

CHAPTER NINE

But it is not really legend that is important for us; it is history.

—François Mauriac

And he could see the censer at Benediction swinging from its chains, myrrh burning on charcoal, the ciborium beside the tabernacle, beside that the sunburst of the monstrance, which suddenly sent its rays through the walls and ceilings as his voice rose. . . .

—Larry Woiwode

As April moved into May, I sensed that the end of my journey was coming. The appearance of the Lord at the meetings was becoming overwhelming to me. The Lord's appearance always seemed to unleash the tongues. Now, as an observer at this group I had never been driven to amusement or indignation, as many highly educated persons are, by the charismatics' habit of praying aloud in various unintelligible languages. Used to being around religious persons, I found the practice arresting, certainly, but no more contemptible or psychologically suspect than, say, the practice of some old ladies to mumble their rosaries aloud in church or of old priests to mutter to themselves in Latin. So I had let the utterances of Spirit-filled individuals bubble around me, scarce noticed at the Saturday meetings.

But when the Spirit really began to move and the Lord came triumphantly among his people, something special happened with the tongues. Ordinarily at these meetings the tongue-speaking began as the private murmurings of separate individuals whose personal feelings had moved them to prayer. But at the Lord's entrance, all the separate tongue murmurings coalesced, as if to form a vibrant mesh or electrical field of sound.

Then, spontaneously, without direction or signal from anyone—no one would be standing, let alone leading—a great and growing cloud of sound would rise, as if a single source had produced it. The result would not be a chorus, strictly speaking, since there were no chords or any attempt at harmony. The individual voices were each in their own key. No two were even saying the same words.

But the effect would be like the murmur of a million ascending bees. It made one think of radio and movie soundtracks whereon are captured the twits, cries, and dronings of all the night and day creatures of streams and woodlands, sound effects that seem to have been gathered in one's very own out-of-doors.

When the tongues welled up in response to the Lord, I always felt washed and uplifted by their vibrant and curiously thrilling hum. Awe and excitement would grip me. If I closed my eyes I could be once again in that green cathedral of my childhood where the water skippers zigzagged their way along the creeks and the monarchs flexed powdery wings in the sun. God's country.

"How I love the tongues," I wrote to Patricia Young one night in early May, "the most beautiful sound I know!" The strange chorus of tongues would always recede just as mysteriously as it had come on, and especially spirited prophecies and hymns of praise would follow.

Prophecies at these prayer meetings had a way of always being called out by persons I could not see who were at some distance from me. A single lifted voice would assert itself from a number of rows behind me or from far across the room. Never, it seemed, would either the Spirit-filled one who gave the prophecy in a tongue or the equally Spirited translator who gave its equivalent a few seconds later in English be sitting right by me.

So too it was with the introductions of the hymns. Someone somewhere in the room would be moved to sing the first line of a hymn aloud and others would automatically join in.

Thus did the old hymn "Holy God" re-enter my life in a dramatic way. It was the last of several hymns of praise that welled up one night in response to the Lord's appearance. The group sang the stirring martial round "Rejoice in the Lord Always" and then, as if inspired by one mighty soul, swung into the majestic eight-fold "Alleluia" that I have since discovered to be a staple with charismatics everywhere.

The room was alive with what felt like an electrical charge. The chorus of tongues had generated it, and the hymns were sustaining it. A man's lone baritone somewhere far behind me boomed into this atmosphere, "Holy God, we praise thy name. . . ."

The effect was immediate. All rose. I was in the act of registering with some surprise that stolid old "Holy God" was indeed a hymn of *praise*, and instinctively I rose up with them.

As if a wall of water had fallen, came the surge, the shower, the cascade of visions. It might have been the close of Benediction, but it seemed more like the opening of Forty Hours. There was the Real Presence, right before our eyes. The glittering monstrance rested high. The priest and attendant servers were rigid in attention.

Roses and fern in great sprays rose on either side like colored fires, and the coiling cloud of rising incense made it all ghostly, like a dream. The congregation shook the rafters:

> *Lord of all, we bow before thee.*
> *All on earth thy scepter claim.*
> *All in heaven above adore thee.*

As they boomed it, there came flooding up at me hugely out of the time corridor not only all the sights and sounds and loved familiar voices of my childhood, but those from a hundred faith-nourishing experiences since. The tunnel of my life itself seemed to have disappeared, dashed away on all sides with the force of my past and present rushing together. All walls around me had spilled away. I saw with perfect clarity the physical settings and details of my numerous encounters with grace—not just churches but playgrounds and classrooms, rectory parlors, a Catholic youth center in Peoria, friends' homes, a women's boarding college with its dorm and library and shrine, a great old university in a grand historic city.

Dear familiar presences, of good relatives and nuns and priests whom I had loved over a lifetime, and who had lavishly loved me, crowded around me where I stood. They assumed the aspect of a protective circle. Their fond faces pressed—I saw my Jesuit mentor's among them —and seemed to ask, "If God had not loved you, would *we* have been there?"

Ringed by this loving company, I made a triumphant grab at reality and pinned it everlastingly down. I *knew* that the Lord truly was, and that he was among us, and that he loved me. *And I too praised*.

That is all. The moment of revelation that I have described here is several years old now. But I still live in the glow of it, and the glow increases in intensity with each passing day.

But now I understand a little better—my logical and analytical mind is still questing—what precisely it was that brought me to my moment of exaltation, of *Benedicite*. I figured it out while rereading Carothers' book about praise. The explanation was so simple, once I saw it, that I wanted to throw back my head and laugh.

In a flash I understood why those hymns of praise, chiefly those, had affected me so strangely at the meetings. They had awed and enchanted me, soothed me, at times virtually ravished me. It would not be wrong to say they had wooed me.

Of course. For our loving God dwells, is warmly and radiantly present, *lives* in the praises of Israel.

> *Yet, Holy One, you*
> *who make your home in the praises of Israel,*
> *in you our fathers put their trust,*
> *they trusted and you rescued them. . . .*
>
> —Psalm 22:3–4

"Holy God, we praise thy name. . . ." And I praise too. I finally do.